Let your love be like the misty rain,
     coming softly,
     but flooding the river.

African Proverb

Once the Wheel of Love has been set in motion,
     there is no absolute rule.

Kama Sutra

O Lord, give me chastity and continence,
     but not yet.

St. Augustine

F: Brings in the "beloved." Honors our loving essences.

M: I like the centered contact of our hands.

F: It's nice to get in touch with your lover and feel the energy flow between you.

M: In this position sometimes I will "caress" the energy emanating from my lover's navel area. For me, this position brings forth the power of the woman and the beauty of the man.

F: Really nice position to abide in . . . using sexual energy generated to bring healing and balancing to each other.

Source: SwiftDeer, Quodoushka

Secret SEXUAL POSITIONS

Ancient
Techniques
For
Modern
Lovers

by
Kenneth Ray Stubbs, Ph.D.

Illustrated by
Kyle Spencer

Secret Garden
Tucson, AZ

Also by Kenneth Ray Stubbs, Ph.D.

Erotic Massage: An Illustrated, Step-by-Step Manual for Couples

Sacred Orgasms: Teachings from the Heart

Tantric Massage: An Illustrated Manual for Meditative Sexuality

Sensual Ceremony: A Contemporary Tantric Guide to Sexual Intimacy

Romantic Interludes: A Sensuous Lovers Guide

The Clitoral Kiss: A Fun Guide to Oral Sex, Oral Massage, and Other Oral Delights

Published by   Secret Garden Publishing
                 5631 W. Placita del Risco
                 Dept. SS
                 Tucson, Arizona 85745

Illustrations: Kyle Spencer
Cover Photo: David Thorpe
Cover Design: Richard Stodart
Author's Photo: Jim Dennis
Illustrator's Photo: Jim Dennis

ISBN 0-939263-15-7

A Word of Caution

The purpose of this book is to educate. It is not intended to give medical or psychological therapy. Whenever there is concern about physical or emotional illness, a qualified professional should be consulted.

All the sexual positions, rituals, and activities in this book are not for every body. Some of the positions were accomplished only after years of yogic practice.

Because of the absurdity of the litigation-happy times in which we live, here is the seemingly necessary legal disclaimer:

The author, illustrator, and publisher shall have neither liability nor responsibility to any person or entity with respect to any loss, damage, injury, or ailment caused or alleged to be caused directly or indirectly by the information or lack of information in this book.

So take responsibility for your own health. Please don't get stuck in a position you can't get out of.

F: I always feel like the Goddess in this position, invoking beauty and love and pleasure into our lives.

M: A great beginning.

F: A sense of togetherness and total bliss.

F: For when you want to guide your man's cock inside of you or tease him by rubbing the head of his cock against your clit.

F: Empowering position for me, and my beloved enjoys the opportunity to also receive. We can maintain eye contact, and our hands are free for caressing or clitoral stimulation.

F: We love to take turns giving and receiving touch, energy, and love.

F: Absolutely eargasmic!

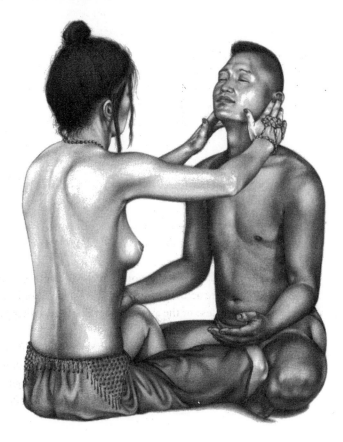

F: I like this one when I want to kiss for hours. Even if he's not completely hard and inside me, this is still very satisfying just to feel him holding me like this.

F: The Royal Yab-Yum. Perfect for allowing male/female energies to interweave, intertwine, and rise through the chakras, deepening bliss and understanding. Good position for heartfelt communications; a sweet daily ritual for beginning or ending the day. Good for working with the breath to bring about full-body orgasm.

M: I love this with circular breathing and eye gazing.

F: A practical point: Supporting the woman with pillows can make it easier on the man's legs, which sometimes go to sleep.

Contents

Chronology of Events   9

Introduction   11

The Wheel of Love   17

Ancient Lovers   27

Modern Lovers   47

The Secrets   79

Selected Positions from the *Kama Sutra*   83

Selected Positions from the *Perfumed Garden*   85

Selected Positions from the *Ananga-Ranga*   95

Selected Positions from the *Ishimpo*   101

India Temple Walls   105

Japanese Shunga Art   123

Appendix: General Thoughts from Readers   135

About the Author and the Artist   136

Some Additional Reading   137

End Notes   139

Acknowledgments   141

F: Fun for playing around.

M: I can only do this for three or four seconds.

F: I think it would take a male gymnast to do this one.

Chronology of Events

• *B.C.E.* means *Before Common Era* and is the same as B.C.
• *C.E.* means *Common Era* and is the same as A.D.
• *c.* means *approximate date.*

c. 3500 B.C.E.	Possible beginning of Inanna legend in Sumer area.
c. 2700 B.C.E.	Possible birth time of the probably mythical Chinese Yellow Emperor, to whom much of the information in the Chinese sex manuals as well as the Japanese *Ishimpo* is often attributed.
c. 2000 B.C.E.	Abraham's birth; father of Judaism, Christianity, and Islam. Born in Sumer area.
c. 1750 B.C.E.	Inanna legend written down on cuneiform tablets in Sumer (at least the tablets used for translation here).
c. 1050 B.C.E.	Solomon reigns over an empire and a harem of possibly up to 700 wives and 300 concubines. Possibly writes the biblical Song of Songs.
c. 800 B.C.E.	In India, Shvetaketu summarizes the "rules of love," which are later distilled and compiled, eventually becoming the *Kama Sutra*.
c. 563 B.C.E.	Siddhartha Gautama, the Buddha, born in northern India.
c. 400–200 B.C.E.	Beginnings of Taoism as a system of philosophy in China. Chuang-tzu and Tao Te Ching, early Taoist books, written.
7–4 B.C.E.	Jesus born, estimated dates.
c. 200 C.E.	Beginning of Tantra movement in India.
c. 300–400 C.E.	*Kama Sutra* written by Vatsyayana in India, various estimated dates of writing. Alain Daniélou, with a new translation in 1994, places the writing during the fourth century C.E., and the texts from which the *Kama Sutra* is compiled going back to at least the third century B.C.E., with an earlier source work coming from Shvetaketu in the eighth century B.C.E.
c. 570 C.E.	Mohammed born.
984 C.E.	*Ishimpo* written by Tamba Yasuyori in Japan: a compilation of many earlier Chinese writings with Taoist influences.
c. 1000 C.E.	Khajuraho temples built in India, with some of the finest erotic sculpture in the world.
c. 1200 C.E.	*Ananga-Ranga* written by Kalyana Malla in India.
1231, 1251 C.E.	Formal beginnings of the Christian Inquisitions, lasting over 500 years.
c. 1250 C.E.	Konarak temples constructed in India, displaying extensive erotic sculpture.

c. 1500 C.E.	*The Perfumed Garden* written by Sheikh Nefzawi in North Africa.
1660-1860 C.E.	Japanese shunga art style flourishes, displaying uninhibited sex.
1848 C.E.	John Humphrey Noyes establishes the Oneida Community in upstate New York and writes *Male Continence*.
1870 C.E.	*Ishimpo* rediscovered by the Chinese in Japan.
1883 C.E.	*Kama Sutra* translated into English.
1885 C.E.	*Ananga-Ranga* translated into English.
1886 C.E.	*The Perfumed Garden* translated into English.
1890 C.E.	Sir Richard Francis Burton dies and his wife immediately burns most of his unpublished erotological translations and writings.
1896 C.E.	Alice Bunker Stockham, M.D., writes *Karezza: Ethics of Marriage*.
1933 C.E.	Nazis burn books and records from the prominent Institute for Sexology in Berlin.
1948 C.E.	Kinsey's *Sexual Behavior in the Human Male* published.
1953 C.E.	Kinsey's *Sexual Behavior in the Human Female* published.
1960s C.E.	Birth control pill popularized.
1966 C.E.	Masters and Johnson's *Human Sexual Response* published.
1968 C.E.	*Ishimpo*'s section on sexuality translated into English as *The Tao of Sex*.
1970 C.E.	Masters and Johnson's *Human Sexual Inadequacy* published.

Introduction

Sex is good.

Sex is holy.

Celebrate it!

This is the teaching of many civilizations.

From thirteenth-century India on the temple walls of Konarak, we easily see life-size stone carvings revealing women and men in almost every conceivable sexual position.

From the *Ishimpo* (ee shem' poh), a thousand-year-old Japanese medical text, we are instructed in a healing sexual position named The Wild Horse Leaps, where the female's feet are lifted toward the heavens and the jade stalk is inserted deeply into the jade gate.

From the biblical Song of Songs, often attributed to Solomon, we glean a hint of the pleasures of oral-vaginal sex—a thousand years before Christianity: "I am my beloved's, and my beloved is mine: he feedeth among the lilies."[1]

From the early sixteenth-century North African Arabic world, we read *The Perfumed Garden*: "Let praise be given to God that He has created woman with her beauty and appetizing flesh: that He has endowed her with hair, waist, and throat, breasts that swell, and amorous gestures which increase desire.[2] . . . God has granted us the kiss on the mouth, the cheeks and the mouth, as also the sucking of luscious lips, to provoke an erection at a favorable time."[3]

From the nineteenth-century Oneida Christian commune in New York State, we learn of *karezza* (kuh ret' zah), where sexual partners lay in coital embrace for an hour with little or no movement, gently riding the passion waves, allowing the sexual energy to build and nurture both their individual and collective body, mind, and spirit.

To many other peoples of many other times, the intertwining of sin and sex would appear strange, perhaps primitive, even heretical.

Sex is primordial. Sexual energy is sacred. Sexual pleasure is healing and transformative. These conceptions were inherent in the worldview of many ancients.

Secret Sexual Positions: Ancient Techniques for Modern Lovers is an introduction to the ancient lover. Drawing from a variety of sources, the following pages take us to methods and philosophies that can open us up to forgotten or undiscovered sensations and feelings, to a more profound sexuality.

Most of the images are based on paintings or written descriptions from India, China, and Japan. Some of the methods go back to very early writings. Some come to us from the probably mythical Chinese Yellow Emperor and his three wise-woman sexual mentors of possibly 5,000 years ago. Actually, in all likelihood, most of the sexual methods here antedate recorded history, for our sexuality is inherent.

The text is intended as an overview rather than an in-depth scholarly treatise. Some of the translations and historical dates are debatable, though they begin to give us meaningful glimpses of other cultures and times.

While much of the available ancient lover material often assumes a male reader and a male being the directing partner, the underlying tone is usually far more egalitarian, sensual, and empathetic than much of the sexually explicit material generated in the West for centuries.

A complete set of sexual positions is far from the goal here. This is a fun book to contemplate possibilities from ancient lovers, human beings who came before us, sought, and discovered.

Feel free to explore this book randomly or to read from cover to cover.

The Illustrations

Four different artistic styles present the variety of human sexual expression here.

First comes illustrations based on photographs of modern lovers interpreting the writings and paintings from ancient lovers. Several of the people in these images are quite accomplished in yoga, as can be seen in the flexibility required in some of the positions. Most of the lovers are experienced in different forms of meditation, as seen in their eye connections.

Next come a large set of line drawings to show a wide variety of positions. These are intended to simply convey the sexual position itself with a hint of the garments, accessories, and environment of some ancient lovers.

Accompanying these two sets of illustrations are quotes from modern lovers. Originally, I asked only lovers proficient in various forms of meditative sexuality, such as Tantra, to write down their experiences in doing or considering doing the position in each image. "Be playful, be serious, be contemplative, be humorous, be critical as you wish. Tell the positive and the negative," I requested.

As others heard about the book in progress, several became intrigued in seeing the images and sharing their comments. In the end, these "quotable quotes" come from friends, relatives, a human sexuality class at a university in Oklahoma, a men's consciousness group in North Carolina, and several experienced porn stars and sexworkers as well as the original group.

Most of the following illustrations depict female-male interactions. Many of the positions can be adapted for female-female and male-male partners, and so several of the quotes are from same-gender lovers.

In the quotes beside the illustrations, an *F* or an *M* indicates a female or male commentator. Noticeably more *F*s appear since more women wrote responses. (The Appendix presents several comments on the general process of viewing and trying out the different positions.)

The next set of illustrations comes from famous sculptures on temple walls in India. While an embarrassment to some contemporary puritanical Indians, these sculptures are among the finest erotic art in the world.

Finally, the classic Japanese erotic art style known as *shunga* gives us a refreshingly different view of sexual positions.

While coming to us mostly from writings and art over many centuries and many cultural milieus, all the illustrations here are from one artist, Kyle Spencer. In each of the four sets, she used a different drawing style. Often the positions included are the result of my instruction to her to have fun with this

project of 100 illustrations. I encouraged her to vary patterns in garments, envision new settings, and basically to follow her artistic heart.

My suggestion to the viewer is the same: Have fun. Open the imagination. Explore the possibilities.

Most of all, allow yourself to experience the beauty and the pleasure of your body which is a temple for the soul.

F: It's kind of a variation on the wheelbarrow
    position. Simple, easy, a whole lot
    less work for the man.

F: Great, effortless penetration for the
    woman. You can just hug a
    pillow and let the man do
    the work; let him go as
    fast or as slow as he
    desires, or tell him
    what you want.

F: This is when I enjoy my partner's "dance" for me . . . enjoy watching and feeling his body of strength and grace. The hands over the heart help me to focus there a bit, thus spreading the pleasure throughout my body.

F: Can't seem to get enough friction or penetration in this position.

F: This position does not allow me to move with my partner.

F: Feeling the heartbeat reminds us of our connection to one another.

F: Looks like the common exercise commandment: Always stretch before a workout.

F: Nope, can't get my leg up that high.

F: This position seems to work best when the partners are similar in height.

F: Looks like you'd pull a leg muscle, but the leverage works wonders!

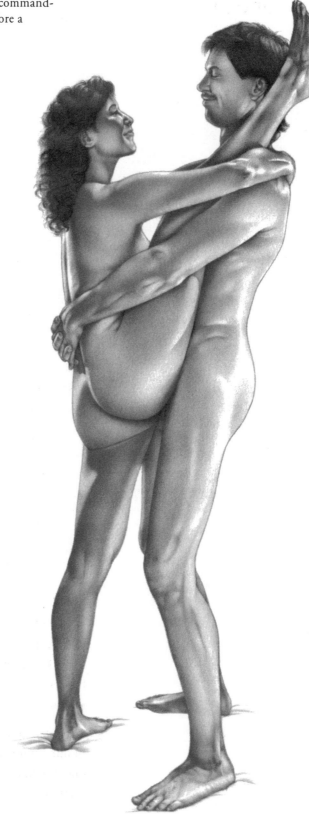

The Wheel of Love

"Once the wheel of love has been set in motion, there is no absolute rule." Thus the *Kama Sutra* reminds us as it instructs in its sixty-four arts of love and sex.

Similarly as for ancient lovers, the wheel turns today for us, modern lovers in a technological, rapid-pace world.

We turn the corner and our eyes connect with someone new . . . for the first time we touch a long-time, platonic acquaintance . . . at a class reunion we reconnect with our long-lost high school sweetheart . . . we are having sex with a just-a-one-night-stand, someone we met at an outdoor café on vacation down in the islands. . . .

And suddenly we realize something is different. We feel it in our chest, maybe our abdomen, our pelvis. It's mutual. We hold each other closely—psychically, energetically, if not physically.

It's chemistry! It's electric! It's intense. The world, our body, is vibrant. We probably call it love, whether we are in puberty or in a rocking chair.

A wheel has been set in motion. An inspiring archetype, the wheel symbolizes wholeness, continuity with the past and the future embraced in the moment. As we fall in love, the wheel consumes us. We soar outside the domain of rules, of techniques, of how-tos, for the wheel of love can take us to both our deepest and to our expanded highest self as well as to our craziest moments.

Dancing in life with the wheel of love in our center, our body and our spirit are as one. We know where and when to touch. We know when to approach, when to wait, when to yield to our beloved's subtle glance. . . .

There are many variations on this theme. We've all probably experienced this more than once, perhaps for a fleeting moment, perhaps for a few weeks, perhaps with the same person at various times throughout much of our lifetime.

❦

Such an interpretation of the wheel of love is real, though rather overromanticized.

This I realized when I finally went all the way.

I was twenty, working as a driver, go-for, general counselor, and bugle boy playing taps at bedtime and reveille at sunrise live for a camp. This was an out-in-nature summer alternative for a culturally and economically diverse group of inner-city Philadelphia kids.

It was a great summer job, away from the mental stresses of college. No calculus or 7:30 A.M. French grammar allowed in these rolling rural hills. The scent of dew-dripped green grasses filled my senses as I prepared for the rapid shrills on my brass cornet, announcing to those mischievous, wonderful little brats that another day of nature walks, swimming, chow, and no fistfights was about to besiege them.

Mary, who was two years older than I, also worked at the camp. One day early in the summer, she came into the small workshop area where I was straightening up. As she reached past me to pick up something, her breasts brushed across my back. I was surprised, pleasantly so. The workshop was small, though I didn't consider it cramped.

She said nothing as she left.

Several days passed—and many fantasies—before I could muster up enough nerve to ask her about her obvious touch. We had barely spoken before. Moreover, she was in a relationship, I thought.

She and her partner had an open sexual relationship, she explained. Their faithfulness agreement included the possibility of having sex with others—these were the first days of *the pill* and the beginnings of the sexual revolution.

My body, however, was still rather inexperienced in the many ways of love and lovemaking other than kissing. Back in high school, my girlfriend and I had only petted, to my great frustration. I would have felt very guilty forcing her to do what she felt she *shouldn't* do, to do what good girls didn't do in those days. Not that I wasn't horny; I just wasn't pushy when it came to going all the way.

So after our Saturday-night once-a-week date, I would find my teenage body and soul going to bed alone, my hormones screaming . . . and doing just as the Everly Brothers had sung: "Dream, dream, dream / All I have to do is dream."

On several occasions in these Saturday-night dreams, I would have vivid intercourse experiences with someone. The dream sensations on my penis felt very real and exceptionally satisfying. Sometimes a wonderful, actual physical wet dream would accompany. Often awaking in the middle of the night, I would find my body curled into almost a fetal position, my arms and thighs squeezing a pillow.

F: It's a lazy, sexy position, lying on top of my lover, straddling him, looking into his eyes, kissing him, and finally sliding his penis deep inside of me.

M: A delight-filled position for me.

F: I love it when he grabs my ass and squeezes—especially when he's inside me.

F: Heart to heart, Mind to mind, Body to body, It's a love divine. (My Tantra teacher taught me this chant.)

F: Very intimate position . . . enjoy this eye contact and almost full-body touch, not to mention the opportunity for me to explore the more active position in the lovemaking.

This was not a dark night of the soul when an alienated psyche searches for spiritual meaning. This was simply my teenage heart and body seeking connection and communion in a sexually suppressed world.

Talking with Mary, I began to quiver uncontrollably as I heard her announce forthrightly, "I want to have sex with you." Even on this typically hot, muggy East Coast summer evening, my body was shaking as if with chills. For many desperate years I had literally dreamed of this. Now in my twentieth summer, I had just been seduced, and my quite willing virgin body was finally going to go all the way—though not at that moment.

We would have to wait until we were both off duty several days later. Driving over to a nearby park, we could have more privacy.

Well, I couldn't wait. For seven years since puberty I had been driving down the freeway of life with one foot on the brakes.

Two days later we just happen to meet at the upstairs bathroom in the caretaker's house. With no one else around, I encourage, she consents.

The camp director and other staff, however, are bustling around downstairs preparing for lunch while we quickly pull down our jeans. In the cramped hallway, we end up in some sort of a missionary position.

After several tries, I realize I don't know how to get it in. I'm anxious; we might get caught at any moment.

Fortunately, Mary is quite experienced. With her hand, she easily guides my penis

past her vulva. She is also very understanding, allowing my virgin body to come and go in a heated rush, totally unlike the fantasized lover with a slow hand.

Later that night in my cabin bunk bed, I reflect alone. My first intercourse had been disappointing, far less pleasurable than my dream sex of a few years earlier. "What else am I to suspect?" I contemplate. "I didn't know how the fuck to do it. Would we have lost our jobs if we had been discovered? Mary was on bottom, and the old farmhouse plank floor, I'm sure, was uncomfortable for her. It's more mutual passion than romantic love—I don't know; it's all new to me. But we'll be going to the park soon."

With a large, soft blanket neatly folded in the back seat, Mary picks me up in her red Mustang a few days later. In the park we drive around searching for an unobtrusive niche in the woods. Nothing is perfect. Resigning ourselves to chance, as lovers always do in a public park, we pull over and lay out the blanket on the ground. As we begin to remove our clothing, the hum of a car motor approaches in the distance. We jump back into our halfway-off jeans just as the car turns down a side road, most likely also seeking a secluded spot to pursue amorous desires.

After a bit, finally we are naked and settling down on the blanket. Oops, there's a sharp stone. We scoot over a little. Keeping an ear out for motor rumbles, Mary again smoothly slides my erect penis into her naturally lubricated vagina. We start our pelvises pumping. "Damn it!" My hand slaps my back side. The mosquitoes are biting my butt—a definite disadvantage if you're on top in the missionary position. I

F: INTENSE hold on and let go. Strength—not just physical.

M: Amazing with the energy running. The stretched penetration felt as if my penis had slid all the way up inside her.

F: With a flexible, strong lover, this position gave me a feeling of spiraling energy engaging us, dancing with us.

F: The meditation quality here is awesome—directing your energy to the pelvic region and feeling it flow back and forth is almost transcendental.

M: I like to explore the FireBreath while in this position.

Author's Note: In the Native American Quodoushka tradition, the FireBreath is a breathing meditation done alone or with a partner. The process includes an intense breathing pattern, contractions of pelvic muscles, and a focus on connecting the chakras, or energetic centers along the core of the physical-energetic body.

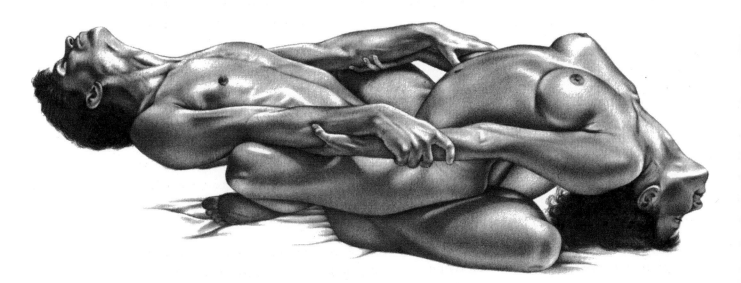

remain undeterred; I've waited too long for this. . . .

❦

Fortunately, that summer I learned more from Mary about sex. Unfortunately, her gift to me was limited mainly to the basics rather than the fine arts. We never had extended privacy. Discreetness had to be our self-imposed prison.

Only many years later did I realize Mary had also given me another gift, a special teaching about honoring one's lover: "My vineyard is mine to give; my fruit is mine to give."[4]

This contemporary translation from the biblical Song of Songs shares a symbolic vision of sexuality so foreign to the principal religious and social tenets dominating much of the world for several millennia. The patriarchal sky-god religions of Judaism, Christianity, and Islam so often relegate the female gender to the role of the ruled if not owned by the male gender. Fortunately, in our techno-modern world, such inveterate misogynous beliefs have far less import today than even only a generation or two ago.

Mary was a sexually liberated woman. Her body was her fruit to share *only* if and when *she* chose. No other male or female could demand that personal choice—influence, maybe; command, no.

I often wonder what would have happened if for my first intercourse I had been with an inexperienced, ambivalent partner? I basically knew only how to kiss and to sometimes undo a bra with one hand. Is this what mutual virgins have to look forward to while holding off till the formal wedding night?

Sex is natural. Sex is inherent in our spiritual being and in our biology, though we know very little of sex naturally.

In the arts of love and sex, we are basically creatures of trial and error. We learn mostly by practicing. We sometimes find an experienced and willing instructor, as I fortunately did in Mary. Sometimes we are the instructor.

Sometimes we learn to dance on the wheel of love through the writings and the art of ancient lovers.

M: Wonderful and easy way for a heart connection.

F: I like the scissoring effect in this position. Plus my lover's hands are free to explore my body and mine his.

F: Be careful in this position: the penis jabbing the ovaries can be painful to the woman.

F: Mmmm, the hand on the heart center helps to spread the energy throughout my body and increase the pleasure all over, not just genitally. Of course, great position for eye contact too.

Source: SwiftDeer, Quodoushka

F: Need to have very flexible legs for this one.

F: This position works very well for orbiting energy and bringing us
    into union. Start at the top of the head and breathe in
    through all the chakra energy centers.

F: My legs go numb after awhile.

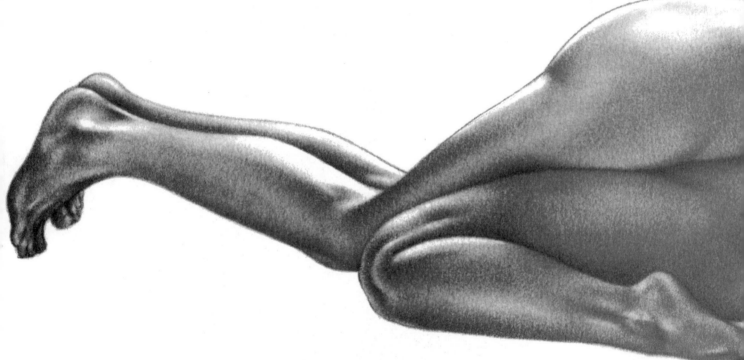

F: Worship her, cherish her, revel in her—she will be
     your reward.

F: Many of the positions in this book translate quite
     well into lesbian positions. My wife and I
     simply see the penises as strap-on dildos.

F: Takes some flexibility, but excellent for opening
     up the whole front of my body, and the
     hand-foot connections feel good. Keeps
     the circuit open for energy to flow
     between the lovers.

F: Like the way the bodies come together and
     touch in such a beautifully
     intricate design.

Ancient Lovers

She went to the sheepfold, to the shepherd. . . .

When she leaned back against the apple tree, her vulva was wondrous to behold.

Rejoicing at her wondrous vulva, . . . Inanna applauded herself.

. . .

As for me, Inanna,

Who will plow my vulva?

Who will plow my high field?

Who will plow my wet ground?

. . .

Who will station the ox there?

Her lover, Dumuzi the King, replies he will.

Then plow my vulva, man of my heart!

Plow my vulva![5]

❧

We gather together to sing praises to our goddess of sex and fertility. She is our source of sustenance. We celebrate her fruition and our future pleasures of the harvest.

Soon we will honor her in ceremony, openly, joyfully, in our yearly *hieros gamos*, the ritualized sacred marriage where our queen and king publicly join in coital union for all of us to observe and give thanks. Sex is our sacrament. Glory be to goddess!

❧

These poetic lines and the hypothetical scenario are historical realities.

A female image as our deity. . . .

Our god having genital congress. . . .

Sex as a sacrament. . . .

Our religious or political leaders performing public sex for us all to view and venerate. . . .

Far from blasphemy, celebrating sexuality and spirituality as an integral whole, a wondrous unity, has been common in various customs for many peoples.

From some of humankind's earliest known writings come the stories and hymns of Inanna. Almost 4,000-year-old cuneiform tablets depict Inanna (ee nah' nuh), the goddess, Queen of Heaven and Earth, as revering her vulva, its beauty, and her sexual desires. Her religious legend, which may go back more than 5,500 years, is from Sumer, a small part of the land area we now generally call the Middle East.

The sacred marriage rite, sometimes public, sometimes private, sometimes only for the religious hierarchy, was (and probably still is) often a sexually consummated ceremony performed by priests and priestesses, or the queen and king, or the whole community. In various cultures around the world, the purpose is to fulfill a religious function, often to please or appease a deity in order to ensure a bountiful crop harvest.[6]

❧

The entangled web of our modern sexual consciousness to a great extent also comes from Sumer, though mostly from a very different religious lineage than Inanna's.

About 4,000 years ago, Abraham, strictly obeying what he believed to be the commands of his god Yahweh, left Ur, once the capital city of Sumer, to find a new land which his "seed" would inherit.

Abraham is the patriarchal progenitor of Judaism, Christianity, and Islam. The religious beliefs and societal laws that have sprung forth from these three pervasive legacies are the foundation of many of the modern lovers' sexual beliefs and customs.

The male gender decides; the female gender follows. Not only are the spirit and the body different; the spirit is morally superior. Pleasures of the flesh are sinful. Sex is solely for procreation. Only the missionary position is condoned. The wages of sin are illness and death.

While many of us modern lovers would contend that most or all of these beliefs are old-fashioned, such tenants remain deeply embedded in our collective unconscious. (Even at the end of the twentieth century, the Chief Justice of the Supreme Court wrote, "Public nudity is the *evil* the state seeks to prevent. . . ."[7] [italics added].)

In contrast, also in the entangled web of our modern sexual consciousness, a compelling anomaly exists among the Jewish and Christian canonized texts. A thousand years after Abraham, Solomon inherited the throne from David to become the most extolled king of Israel. With a probably exaggerated estimate of 700 wives and 300 concubines, Solomon also no doubt had ample opportunity to explore the amatory realms. Often though probably inaccurately attributed to him, the Song of Songs graces our minds with images only lovers would feel:

M: Like to find a lover who could do this!

F: Think you've got to be a gymnast here.

F: This version of 69 is spectacular, but we
   couldn't pull it off. The possibilities
   for orbiting energy were intriguing.

F: I prefer to be in a relaxed position to receive
   and give pleasure.

Source: the demonstrating couple

M: Reminds me of the tenderness of
    making love.

F: This is another version of yab-yum we
    use with reciprocal breathing:
    exhaling out through the heart
    and down the right arm, giving
    love into the partner's heart. In
    the accompanying eye gazing,
    the light of love moves out of
    the right eye into the left eye of
    the beloved, who receives it as
    he inhales the sweetness.

M: Mostly an emotional sharing of energy.

F: Like this one because the legs are relaxed. It's hard to get rapid or long penetration, because your arms are doing most of the work.

F: Wonderful when done slowly.

M: I'm glad that sex isn't just for the youngsters, the fashion models, and the yogic adepts. I appreciate the full range of human body sizes, shapes, and ages.

F: Good position to have lingam/yoni "conversation" by taking turns contracting respective lingam/yoni muscles.

Author's Note: *Lingam* is Sanskrit for penis, and *yoni* is for the female genitals as a whole.

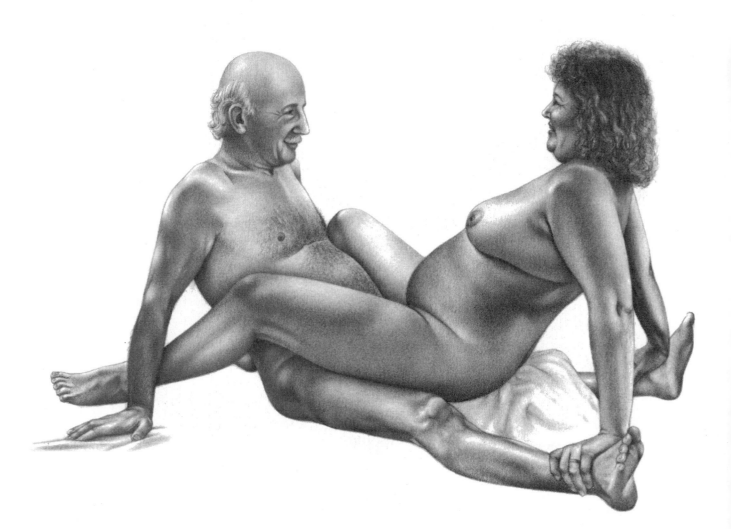

*Let him kiss me with the kisses
of his mouth: for thy love is
better than wine.* [Song of
Songs 1:2]

*A bundle of myrrh is my well-
beloved unto me; he shall lie all
night betwixt my breasts.* [Song
of Songs 1:13]

*I am my beloved's, and his
desire is toward me.* [Song of
Songs 7:10]

These poetic praises from the Song of
Songs, or Song of Solomon, often bear
striking resemblances to Inanna's hymns.
This should be of no surprise. Solomon built
temples for a variety of female and male
deities other than Yahweh, and the Sumerian
civilization was part of his roots.

Solomon's kingdom was a bustling
empire of commerce and far-reaching
alliances bringing cultural contact with those
far beyond a provincial world of sheepherd-
ers and purist priests. Goddess traditions
honoring the cycles of the moon as well as
earth-centered fertility ceremonies celebrating the fecundity of plants, herds, and
humans alike abounded both within the
diverse early Hebrew people and in surrounding cultures.

Nonetheless, a priesthood with a single,
wrathful, male deity was to be the dominating power for the early Hebrews. Even
ethnic cleansing of other male and female
deities' followers, including the slaughter of
all men, women, and children, was not
uncommon.[8] Sometimes, though, the gold,
domesticated animals, and the female
virgins were spared and made property.[9]

The Christianity of Paul (d. 62–68 C.E.)

followed, then the conversion of the Roman
Empire to Christian doctrine (early 4th
century), later the sex-is-sin philosophies of
Augustine (345–430) and Aquinas (1225–
1274). Eventually, either with active promo-
tion or acquiescence from the Church of
Rome or Protestant powers, over 500 years
of formal Inquisitions were to leave little
semblance of spiritual traditions espousing
sex as a sacrament. After perhaps up to nine
million burnings at the stake and other
tortured deaths,[10] European Christendom
had basically committed genocide on those
who would dare to engage in spiritual
practices which Inanna, Astarte, Aphrodite,
and other western European sex-embracing
deities might proclaim.

In the Americas, Balboa would unleash
his large, specially trained attack dogs on
indigenous peoples for their common sexual
customs deemed heretical to the Church of
Rome. Add the influence of the puritanical
wings of the Protestants, and we find the
Western twentieth-century modern lover
inheriting the legacy of a virtual sexual
wasteland.

For almost 4,000 years, our principal
cultural heritage has known and taught little
in the arts of love and sex. Moreover, a
wondrous unity of sex and spirit has been
philosophically unconscionable.

❦

And then there was Sir Richard Francis
Burton.

Burton (1821–1890) was a famous
British explorer and prolific author with
forty-three volumes on his explorations and
almost thirty volumes of translations.

Based on his fluency in forty languages

F: Now here's a man who knows how to make love to a
    woman! Gee, this is my kind of guy!

M: A way to let my lover know that she is safe.

M: Basking in the afterglow, catching one's breath.

F: When we do this, I always feel the central core
    channel flow free and clear like running
    water. It's wonderful after sex and after a
    massage.

Source: Author's tantric massage / erotic massage book;
    similar to karezza methods.

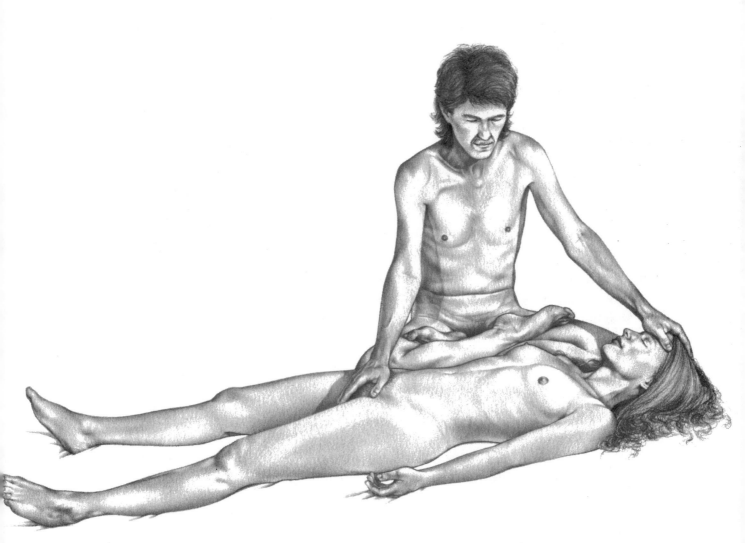

and dialects as well as extensive experiences of "going native" in India and in Muslim cultures, Burton translated and secretly printed the *Kama Sutra* in 1883, the *Ananga-Ranga* in 1885, and *The Perfumed Garden* in 1886. (Often cotranslating with Burton was his close friend Foster Arbuthnot.)

Risking prosecution, imprisonment, and disgrace in Victorian Britain, Burton was a bicultural messenger, clandestinely bringing glimpses of ancient lovers' arts of love and sex long suppressed in the West. Probably more than any other single individual in the English language, Burton lifted the sex-is-sin veil so that we might see a far healthier possibility of our sexual selves.

Kama is the god of love in India. Similar to Cupid, Kama has a bow that shoots love-producing flower arrows. The term *kama* itself can be translated as "love, pleasure, sensual gratification."

A sutra is a collection of concise statements, written so that they might be more easily memorized. In the case of the *Kama Sutra*, scripturelike advice provides guidance not only on succeeding in the arts of love and sex, for which the book is most known, but also on attaining virtue and wealth. Ironically, with sexual censorship waning in the 1960s and various printings of this formerly illicit treasure becoming commonly available, it is the sections on virtue and wealth that are often conveniently edited out.

Writing the *Kama Sutra* somewhere between the fourth century B.C.E. and the fourth century C.E., Vatsyayana described himself in the conclusion of this significant compilation and adaptation of previous writings in India:

> The Kama Sutra *was composed, according to the precepts of Holy Writ, for the benefit of the world, by Vatsyayana, while leading the life of a religious student, and wholly engaged in the contemplation of the Deity.*[11]

Where sexual union can symbolize the union of cosmic energies, it would not seem strange that a holy person could write a text describing the arts of love and sex. Harmony in the universe and harmony between lovers are but a mirror of each other.

Beginning in the third and forth centuries in India, a dynamic spiritual movement known as Tantra (tahn' tra) began to appear. By that time many of the dominant religious themes emphasized asceticism: Only by denying the body and abstaining from pleasure could one lead a holy life. Suffering and penance, including self-inflicted pain, were next to godliness.

Tantra, to an ascetic, might be considered hedonistic indulgence. For a Tantric adept, all of life and death is embraced. Every experience, especially sex, is an opportunity to discover more deeply our inherent nature.

Various meditations, including sexual ceremonies and positions, some apparently adapted from the *Kama Sutra* information, were developed to teach the follower on this path. Through meditation, our experience of daily existence—the good, the bad, the ugly, the beautiful—is transformed from attachment to enlightenment.

Tantra, indeed, is a path, often requiring many years of commitment to various meditations, or "surrender to," as a Tantrika might conceptualize it. This path is for those seeking more than a new romantic or sexual skill. Nonetheless, this diverse philosophy, which has had significant influences on Hinduism and Buddhism, gives us some insight into the ancient lovers' embrace of the sacred and the sexual, a view far outside the sex-is-sin perversion pervading our Western sexual legacy.

(*Tantra*, the term, appears increasingly in book and video titles for the modern lover. Some suggest, though, *Neo-Tantra* would be a more appropriate term as tantralike methods are adapted and developed for the Western mind and body.)

In late twelfth-century India, the *Ananga-Ranga*, or, *The Hindu Art of Love* was written by Kalyana Malla. Arriving after Islamic conquerings and cultural influences, this book, however, is derived from the *Kama Sutra*. Emphasizing a marriage relationship, the manual accentuates the mutual pleasure and harmony of the genders:

> *And thus all you who read this*
> *book shall know how delicious*
> *an instrument is woman, when*
> *artfully played upon; how*
> *capable she is of producing the*
> *most exquisite harmony; of*
> *executing the most complicated*
> *variations and of giving the*
> *divinest pleasures.*[12]

The third of Burton's translations, *The Perfumed Garden* by Sheikh Nefzawi, comes to us from the Islamic culture in early sixteenth-century North African Arabic Tunis. Here again pleasure more than procreation is praised:

> *If you wish to experience an*
> *agreeable copulation, one that*
> *gives equal satisfaction and*
> *pleasure to both parties, it is*
> *necessary to frolic with the*
> *woman and excite her with*
> *nibbling, kissing, and caressing.*
> *Turn her over on the bed,*
> *sometimes on her back, some-*
> *times on her belly, until you see*
> *by her eyes that the moment of*
> *pleasure has arrived. . . .*[13]

No slam-bam-thank-ya-ma'am aura is exalted in these treatises translated by Burton, except, of course, when such encounters are mutually rewarding for both partners.

Looking to the ancient lovers farther east in China and Japan, we often find more of a medical emphasis in the numerous sexual texts, such as the twenty-eighth section of the Japanese *Ishimpo*. This is a compilation and adaptation of many earlier Chinese texts often extensively influenced by Taoist spiritual philosophy. (Tao is pronounced *dow*, like wow beginning with a d.)

> *One gets longevity by loving*
> *the essence, cultivating the*
> *spiritual, and partaking of*
> *many kinds of medicines; if you*
> *do not know the ways of*
> *intercourse, partaking of herbs*
> *is of no benefit.*[14]

Being in harmony with our inner nature might be considered the quintessence of Taoist philosophy, dating back to at least the fourth century B.C.E. in China. Sexual health is an essential aspect of health if we are to live in balance with Heaven and Earth. So part of a physician's role would be to facilitate our sexuality remaining in harmony with the other aspects of our life—including knowing which sexual positions help heal which conditions.

Also striking to the Western modern lovers' ear is the sensual ambiance of the poetic language describing sex. "The clouds and the rain" and "the mists and the rain" refer to intercourse. A penis is a "jade stalk" or a "bamboo horse." A "pearl on the jade step" is a clitoris, while a "coral gate," "jade pavilion," and "magic field" are the female genitals in general. "Fire inside the jade pavilion" would be a woman's orgasm.

While having many differences, Taoism and Tantra may at first to the Westerner appear woven from the same thread. In both philosophies, pleasure and health can derive from sexuality. Public ceremony celebrating sexuality has been common for some followers in each tradition. Both philosophies have spiritual symbolism displaying the union of complementary opposites, sometimes in human form, sometimes in abstract form. And compared to our patriarchal religions, egalitarian honoring of the masculine and the feminine archetypes is far more obvious.

Moreover, in both traditions, sex is an arena for discovering, developing, and transforming the subtle energies. The *aura, chakras, chi, ki, prana, acupuncture meridians,*

nadis, kundalini, and other energetic terms are typical nomenclature.

In both Tantra and Taoism, we are more than a physical body. We are also mystical beings. Here, though, our sexuality is an essential key, rather than an obstacle, to the mystical gateway.

The Americas provide the final two main ancient lover sources for *Secret Sexual Positions.*

Karezza is Italian for "a caress." Karezza, the sexual method, however, is an American development from the mid-nineteenth century.

After leaving Yale Divinity School, John Humphrey Noyes (1811–1886) established the famous Oneida Community in 1848 in upstate New York. Here for over thirty years in a communal environment, until extensive societal pressure forced a cessation of their sexual lifestyle, the participants were to practice lovemaking in a manner many might find unconventional.

About eighty years after karezza's introduction, one of its proponent's described the approach for a male partner:

> *Try to feel yourself a magnetic battery, with [your penis] as the positive pole, and pour out your vital electricity to her and consciously direct it to her womb, her ovaries, her breasts, lips, limbs, everywhere—filling her in every nerve and fiber with your magnetism, your life, love, strength, calmness, and peace.*[15]

F: I've done this on a chaise lounge and it gives the legs and arms, amongst other things, a great workout!

M: I like the rear view and the female being active.

F: This one makes me feel very dominant, standing over a man. The key here is to find the right height couch to do it on!

F: But I don't think my coffee table is sturdy enough.

F: Easy to balance; good for longer duration.

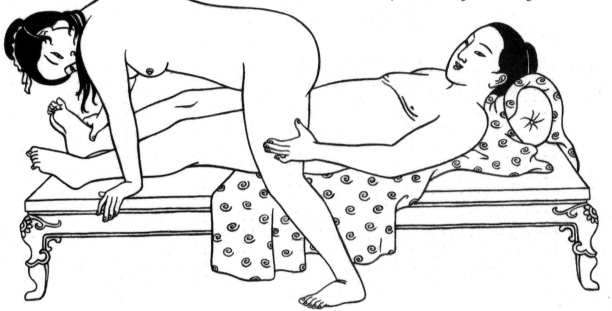

F: Great for deep penetration!

M: A gift of visual pleasure when a female gives me such an extreme view.

F: Wow! Definite orgasm.

F: When I want to show my heart's full of love by giving to my partner this "dance of love" on his lingam. Our eye contact deepens the intimacy.

M: My favorite way to slide up and down his penis.

F: Here he can also use his fingers to stimulate my clit.

M: I love the hands pressing together.

F: Great with a lover who has an erection that stands straight up against his stomach.

F: With my legs closed, it makes it more intense for both my lover and me to feel each
       other. The arms outstretched and the closeness is very intimate and loving.

M: The key here is stillness, eye contact, and breathing.

F: A lover's look, a lover's hold; sweet, sweet kisses, and then we mold.

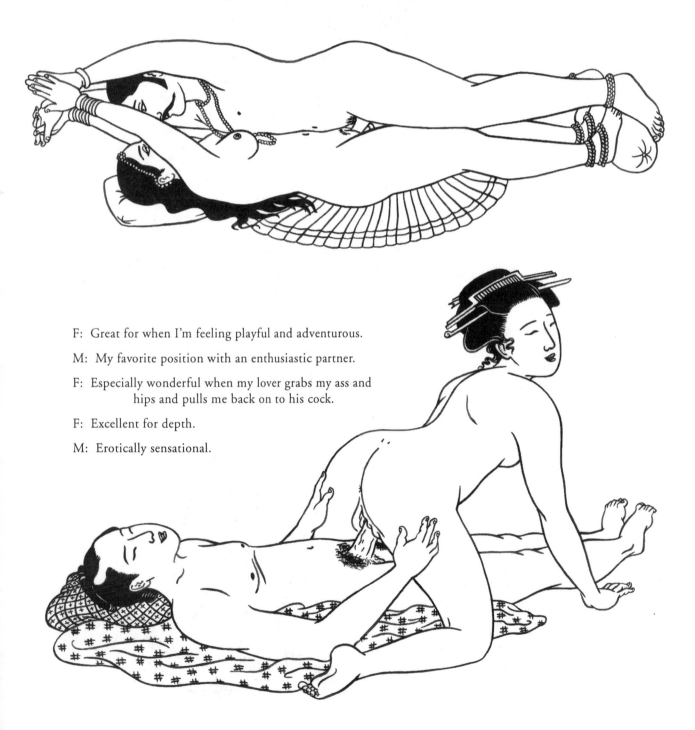

F: Great for when I'm feeling playful and adventurous.

M: My favorite position with an enthusiastic partner.

F: Especially wonderful when my lover grabs my ass and
       hips and pulls me back on to his cock.

F: Excellent for depth.

M: Erotically sensational.

F: Great for fun in the water. The weightless quality allowed a "no-stress" connec-tion!

M: This is great in the heat of passion when there seems to be no time to find the right place.

F: Love this position; it makes me feel so submissive. My lover starts sitting down with me straddling him. When the time is right, he stands up, grabs me with his arms, and lowers me up and down his cock. All I can do is hang on for ecstasy.

F: I have been put against a wall or door where my one leg was down and the other up around my lover's waist. It's a very submissive position and I love the power my lover has over me while I'm pinned against the wall and him.

F: It's hard to do, but well worth the workout. Can be made easier by using a wall.

In karezza, generally, partners would lie in coitus for perhaps an hour with little or no movement. So as to build up the energetic charge, the male was to refrain from ejaculating except when intending procreation (similar to the Taoist approach). The female partner could have orgasms, though monitoring her actions in order not to overstimulate her partner to the point of ejaculation.

Noyes called this method *male continence*, which is also the title of his out-of-print 1848 book. *Karezza*, coined by Alice Bunker Stockham, M.D. (1833–1912), however, was to become the method's more widely known title.

Stockham was one of the first five women to receive an M.D. in America. She would later be arrested for distributing birth control information (condoms were illegal then); travel to India and study Tantra with a matriarchal culture; and almost fifty years after Noyes's *Male Continence*, write *Karezza: Ethics of Marriage*, another usually out-of-print book.

Contrasting with Noyes on some of the specifics of the method, Stockham felt the benefits gained by a male in refraining from ejaculation would be equally beneficial for a female if she were to refrain from her own orgasm as well.

Regardless of which karezza school of thought one followed, the main purposes were to have an intimate and loving relationship along with radiant physical and emotional health.

Quodoushka (kwah doesh' ka) comes to us from Turtle Island, the name given to North, Central, and South America by some of the peoples who have lived here for millennia.

In the Quodoushka cosmology, the human being is conceptualized from the sacred circle with the four directions. In the north is the mental. In the south is the emotional. In the west is the physical. In the east is the spiritual.

In the circle's center is the catalyst. Here is where our sexuality resides. At the core of our nature, sexuality gives birth to the aspects of our humanity.

The full name for these teachings is Chuluaqui (chu' la quay) Quodoushka. *Chuluaqui* could be translated as the primordial life force energy. Without this energy, there would be no form or substance in the universe.

Quodoushka could be interpreted as sacred sexuality. It is sexual union in the broad sense of mental, physical, emotional, spiritual, and sexual harmony.

This harmony can be realized with or without genital contact, with an ongoing lover or a total stranger or a nonsexual friendship. It might be in an intellectual discussion, a flirtation, a platonic hug, or in passionate lovemaking. The connection could be with oneself, another or others, an animal or a plant, even with an energetic field in nature.

This may appear rather foreign to those of us growing up in the Judeo-Christian framework, where sex and spirit are philosophically in conflict.

Sexuality as a path to our soul: This is the conceptual shift modern lovers must make to understand many of the ancient lovers' philosophies.

To make this shift, we must openly embrace our senses and our body in its natural state.

F: Getting into this position started us laughing, turned into fun for the sake of fun.

F: My lover has a "pillow room," a chamber, almost like a Sultan's, with lots of pillows, soft fabrics, and a stereo. We use this to really get comfortable in our many positions like this one.

M: I like how they're both sitting upright with his legs around hers.

F: A great position for eye gazing—for union through the windows of the soul while joining the sexual centers.

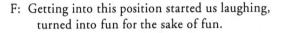

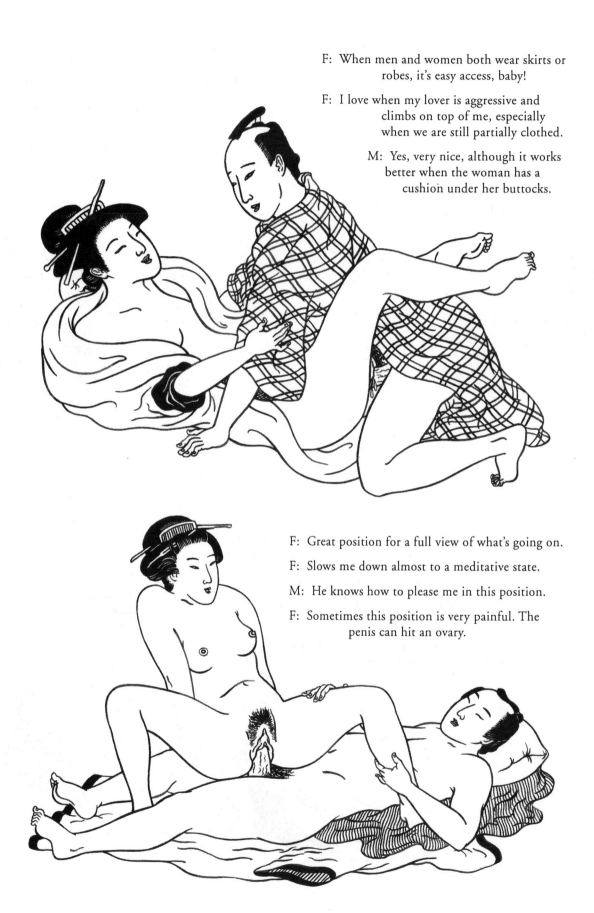

F: When men and women both wear skirts or
   robes, it's easy access, baby!

F: I love when my lover is aggressive and
   climbs on top of me, especially
   when we are still partially clothed.

M: Yes, very nice, although it works
   better when the woman has a
   cushion under her buttocks.

F: Great position for a full view of what's going on.

F: Slows me down almost to a meditative state.

M: He knows how to please me in this position.

F: Sometimes this position is very painful. The
   penis can hit an ovary.

F: With some maneuvering it can be a very intense G-spot pleaser.

F: This one with my girlfriend takes me over the edge every time.

F: Only works for me with a partner who has a downward or semierect erection.

M: Wonderful having her feet available.

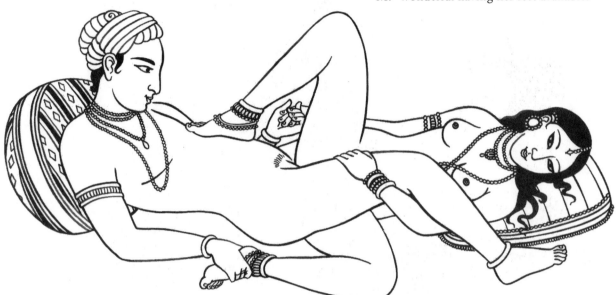

F: One of my favorite positions—basic missionary only with my partner hands under my upper back, holding me tight.

F: Very intimate contact gives each of us a loving feeling.

M: For me, the traditional missionary position sometimes leads to neck strain.

F: One of our favorites—especially when he whispers something nasty in my ear!

F: This is one of my all time favor-
    ites—especially wearing
    spiked heels and sexy
    lingerie. Being able to
    really hold and caress his
    penis and balls sends us
    both into waves of
    ecstasy.

F: What a nice way to start the
    evening! Gets our
    attention.

F: Love this one: sucking cock
    in a submissive
    position. This
    one's even
    comfortable, and
    I can stimulate
    myself while I'm
    sucking him.
    This really gets
    me horny just
    thinking
    about it.

M: Yummy!

F: I love swing sex. I've screwed on playground swings and in bondage swings but never in a contraption like this, but I'm looking for one.

M: I'm always glad to know that the industrial revolution could serve a higher purpose.

F: My lover is working on a replica, using his sky chair as a model to work from.

M: Where can I order it?

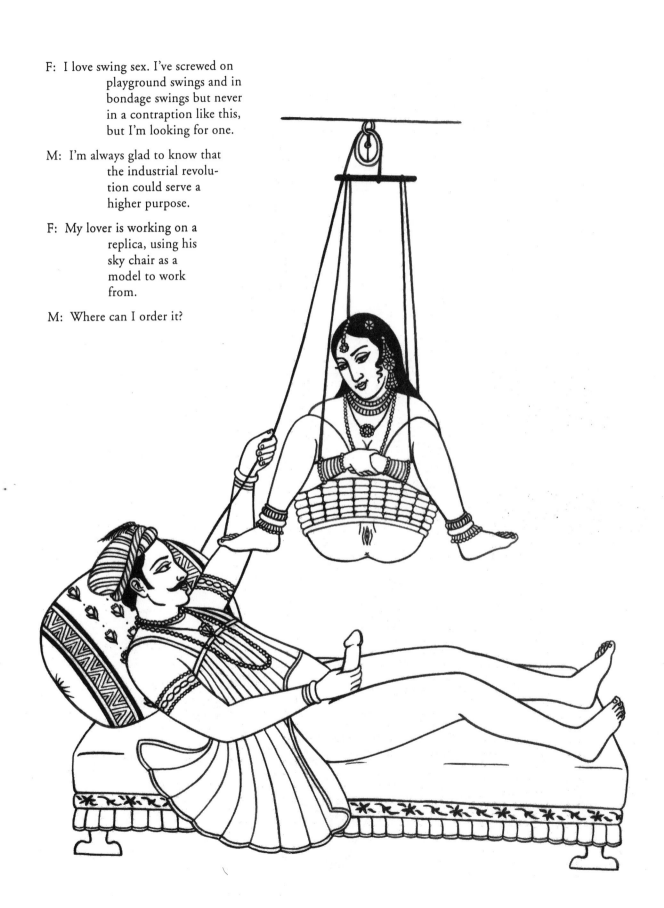

F: Lovely, particularly at sunset. Don't forget cushions for the bottom of the boat.

M: Reminds me of my adolescence in the bayou, but we got to pull the boat up on the bank first.

F: Small boats in particular are challenging. They are not curved in easy ways.

F: You can row, row, row your boat gently down my stream any time you want.

M: Mother told me never to talk with my mouth full; now I know what she's talking about.

F: We love this one—it's erotic for sure! The mutual stimulation, the taste, the scent. . . .

M: What a glorious thing to suck his penis and feel the same on mine.

M: I prefer a pillow under my neck to prevent strain.

Modern Lovers

In clear English with a definite Chinese accent, Dr. Chang was lecturing from behind a short podium in front of the fireplace.

This was multicultural San Francisco in the Mission District, a mainly Hispanic section, only a few blocks from my favorite Mexican restaurant. It was the late 1970s, about fifteen years, many experiences, and many miles from my sexual-novice, modern-lover summer with Mary in the Pennsylvania hills.

A flyer I had seen posted in a local natural foods store had announced Dr. Stephen Chang would be giving a seminar on Taoism and sexuality.

I had read Jolan Chang's (unrelated to Stephen Chang) recently published *Tao of Love and Sex* and had come away eager for more. Finally, a bicultural messenger with a real understanding of ancient Chinese culture had written a comprehensible book for the modern Western world.

When I saw Dr. Stephen Chang's poster, I felt this would be an important opportunity. Being in the presence of an accomplished teacher, we are likely to learn in ways not as accessible while reading a written text, as informative and inspiring as the text may be.

With a live teacher, there can be a transmission of knowledge of other than a cognitive form. And finding a teacher who walks his talk culturally and physically is a rarity.

Dr. Chang's grandmother had been a master physician. His great grandfather had been both a physician to a Chinese empress as well as the first Chinese ambassador to the United Kingdom. Dr. Chang himself is trained in both Chinese and Western medicine and holds degrees in philosophy, theology, and law.

In a typical Taoist manner, Dr. Chang was lecturing without pretentious indications of his extensive background, there in his living room converted into a seminar room. His enthusiasm for the topic, however, was evident.

First, he explained that the ancient Taoists were very practical: If a technique does not work, discard it. Of course, if a method is very foreign to us, we might best explore it long enough to see if it does not really work for us.

Continuing, Dr. Chang discussed the eight pillars of Taoism. These include a balanced diet, the use of healing herbs, the practice of internal exercises such as certain breathing techniques, the healing arts based on the acupuncture meridians, the study of cosmic forces in order to live harmoniously with them, as well as other pillars.

The focus of this weekend, though, was to be the Tao of Sex Wisdom pillar. In his *Tao of Sexology*, he defines this pillar as "the use of sex and sexual energy for improving health, harmonizing relationships, and increasing spiritual realization."[16]

I had already been studying with two accomplished meditation teachers for a few years, including a Tibetan lama. Chang, however, was for me the first to openly teach sexuality as a spiritual meditation.

I was to learn a number of ancient lovers' techniques that weekend. A few I would follow for many years, some having a major impact on my sexual life. Perhaps more important though was the friendship

that was to develop.

On certain days of the week, Stephen held open office, where for no fee anyone could just drop in, discuss philosophical ideas, personal concerns, or purchase hard-to-find Chinese herb blends.

From time to time for over a decade, that's how I continued the contact. We would chat about the books we were each writing and publishing, the seminars we were each teaching around North America and Europe, some of the insights I was gaining.

On my last visit with Stephen before I was to move away from San Francisco, he shared about how he was being allowed to reenter China and teach Taoism to the factory workers and others. A subtle feeling of elation emanated from him. I began to sense the bicultural messenger had come home.

Fortunately, through this connection I had been able to touch and feel and see a philosophy embodied. For me, he had become a cultural bridge between the worlds of the ancient and the modern lovers.

It was as if Stephen had appeared on my path to say, "Ray, look at this. Yes. It *is* possible."

❧

Driving my hippie van into San Francisco from the mountains of Mexico on New Year's Eve, 1972, I had no idea I was also beginning my journey into the ancient lovers' realm—eventually to meet Stephen Chang and other influential teachers.

A few months earlier my lover, Shannon, and I had decided to take separate

M: The view, the erotic feel, and the access to rubbing her legs are all moving.

F: I like the eye-to-eye contact here and my partner's hands on my nipples. Unfortunately, all of my weight is supported on my hands. So I couldn't hold it for long.

M: Had to hold on, kept slipping, which turned into a whole other game.

F: A favorite that gets a lot of really good spots.

F: Pillows under his back are a must.

F: This Hot Seat I like!

paths. We had met two and a half years earlier at a party, and within an hour she had propositioned me to go to bed.

I stuttered back, "But I don't know you." Not that I wasn't interested; I was simply still unaccustomed to such straight-forwardness. A bit later that evening, though, I accepted her invitation. And the wheel of love began turning.

It was chemistry like I had never felt before. Twenty-four hours later I walked home slowly on the snow-packed streets, sore, bowlegged, and very satisfied.

She was a poet, and I was a sociology instructor at the local college. In a few months at the end of the school year, we built a bed platform in my van, loaded a couple of boxes of books and a Coleman stove, and hit the road for two years of new adventures and great sex.

Our motto, simply, was "If this van is rockin', don't bother knockin'." It seemed anything could set our sexual juices flowing. In a twinkling of an eye, we would turn the van into a rest stop, close the curtains, and shake, rattle, and roll.

For most of those two years, we discovered America, Mexico, and each other. We paid our way by planting trees in the Idaho mountains, picking cherries in Montana, driving tractors during apple harvest on the eastern slopes of the Cascades. There was not much gender differentiation here—often working the same jobs, seeing the same eagles, getting the turista together in Mexico.

The sex was very satisfying, even to the end, when we realized we were changing and it was better to part. After apple harvest,

with tears we went our separate ways, Shannon back to New York to become an award-winning poet, me back to the Mexico, seeking god in those ancient, mystical mountains.

I experienced much on that trip to Mexico, but the language barriers were severely limiting. In an Indian village, possibly of Mayan descent, up in the Chiapas mountains accessible only by foot or by horse, all I could do was smile as I looked for the wisdom of their ancestors in the villagers' eyes. We had few common words.

And my body was yearning touch. More than sex, I missed Shannon's embrace and cuddling. Our constant companionship and sexual affinity had not only allowed me to develop into a fairly experienced modern lover but had also taken me into an un-known realm of nurturing.

So, after three months of Spanish road signs and a little over a hundred dollars in my pocket, I headed my van north to San Francisco to study massage, Jungian psy-chology, a Taoist martial art, and other new-to-me consciousnesses.

My first job turned out to be in a porn theater selling tickets, running the projector, being the sex toys buyer, and subbing as candy girl, as the position was labeled. It was all quite new for me. Tits and ass, cocks and cunts, moaning and groaning, fucking and sucking on a large screen—but after about two weeks of my jaw gaping, I became bored to death. It was the same old humpin' and pumpin', just different locations and different faces (close-ups of the genitals usually looked the same).

M: I'm a "bottom guy" and love to rise up on my feet arching my back and pushing against my lover's weight. Bodies close; very fiery for me.

F: Good for when I'm feeling dominant . . . the closeness of leaning down to kiss him, to rub my chest against his while he's deep inside me.

F: When I do this one with my girlfriend for a good length of time, I have a deep "belly-gasm."

F: Good when your lover has a curve in his penis, curving up; or he has an erection that brings his cock straight up against his belly. Either way, in this position the shaft of the cock is rubbing on the clit, which feels great.

F: My legs eventually go numb.

F: Not as difficult as it appears if her pillows are high enough!

F: Is this what I get from yoga lessons?

Yes, women were frequently depicted in a degrading manner, but the male characters were equally degraded. Personally, I found what the TV game show guests were required to do was far more demeaning. Moreover, in the porn movies, the nude body was a much more honest revelation of the person.

Sometimes I've wondered if ancient lovers were to view our porn flicks, would they assume that *coitus interruptus* is standard modern lover behavior? Almost always the male withdraws his penis from the female's vagina, anus, or mouth just in time to eject white globs all over the screen. Absolutely no faked male orgasms here. I didn't, and still don't, understand all the hoopla for and against this low-grade art genre.

When *Deep Throat* was busted in New York's Times Square, the grade-D movie suddenly became a pop phenomenon. In San Francisco, the 800 seats filled up inside the Presidio, the middle-class-neighborhood theater where I worked. Outside sometimes up to 400 were standing in line. Middle America now had permission to see a porn flick and talk about it at the office the next day.

For me, *Deep Throat* turned out to be a turning point. Working lots of extra hours, I finally had enough money to go to massage school.

Studying massage, I found a home. Touch such as I had discovered with Shannon again became accessible. Sex can be very nurturing but not the only meaningful way to find this basic human sustenance, I began to realize.

Learning the anatomy and the kinesiology was valuable, but the hands-on, that was the art and the fun. The massage instructor would demonstrate. Then we'd all take off our clothes; one would jump on the table; and the partner would try out the strokes. I soon learned it was best to practice first and receive second. That way, I could bliss out with lots of yummy feelings without having to think about getting up off the table and coordinating my memory, eyes, and hands in my turn to practice.

Sure, I had done a lot of skinny dipping with other hippies in the lakes and streams across America, but nude classes. . . . It was awkward at first. When you're in a state of bliss, though, the only good reason to put your clothes on was the chilling fog blanketing San Francisco outside.

This massage school was rather avant-garde. The principal massage style taught there had been popularized at Esalen Institute, the grandmother of human potential centers. At Esalen, perched above the Pacific Ocean in the mountains of Big Sur, California, a person would melt in a natural hot springs pool with thousands of stars above, waddle over to an open-air massage table, and with the sounds of crashing waves a couple of hundred feet below, receive an hour of nurturing, long, flowing massage strokes. Clothing, while optional, seemed quite superfluous.

So, in my massage training, we spent about a total of five minutes learning draping, the procedure for covering the client's supposed modest parts with a sheet or

F: Nice for initial connecting with my partner, but there's no really serious in-and-out penetration here.

F: Sit without body movement—touch face with hands—use kegels and abdominal muscles only—wonderful exercise in self-control.

F: Rock-a-bye, baby!

M: This position allows me to be intense. A variation is with the woman's legs on my shoulders or against my chest.

F: Also a nice position for a foot massage.

F: Using her feet, she can get leverage. Plus, he has a great view.

F: Good for deep penetration and the ability to access the clitoris.

M: Great G-spot strokes!

F: Real tight, real deep, and real GOOD.

F: Great variation to the missionary position. I'm lying back very relaxed and somewhat submissive while he caresses my breasts or rubs my clitoris.

F: My cup runneth over.

M: A great buns exercise.

F: A great reason to visit Pakistan.

F: My lover covered a big earth ball with fabric: fun but tricky to stay in one position for long.

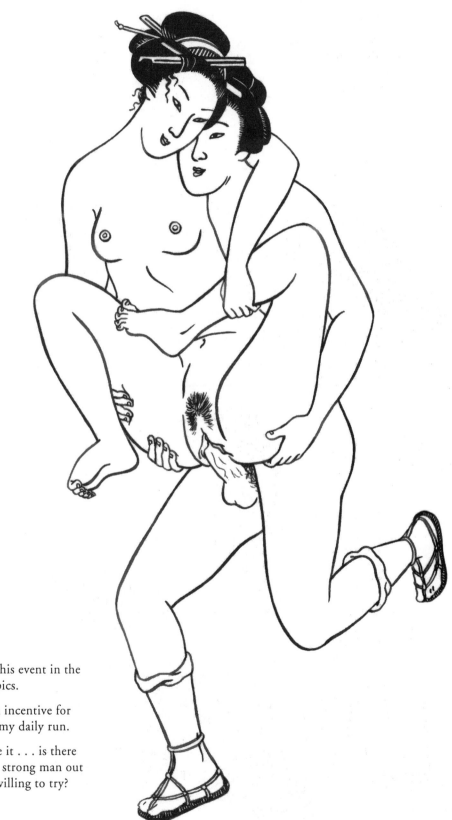

F: I'd like to see this event in the Olympics.

M: Now here's an incentive for doing my daily run.

F: I've never done it . . . is there a nice, strong man out there willing to try?

towel. Of course, the client's comfort level is always the determining factor, but this was San Francisco in the 1970s, a time of rebirth of the human body and spirit. Many were shedding both their emotional and physical garments of the puritanical fashion.

As it turned out, I was a natural in massage. Soon I was out in the world building a massage practice and teaching a few weekend intro classes.

At the same time, a somatic renaissance was occurring. Many styles of massage and bodywork were becoming accessible, some traditional from Asia or Europe, some contemporary innovations. To my repertoire, I added shiatsu, polarity therapy, and reflexology.

Just north of San Francisco, my massage practice at a body center named after a Hindu goddess of healing brought me in contact with other somatic seekers. I rubbed elbows with Rolfers, yoga teachers, tai chi instructors, acupuncturists, and some of the early innovators in the wellness health movement.

Yet one question was rarely explored: What about sex and sexual energy? It's okay for the tears to flow on my massage table. It's okay to pound on pillows to release suppressed anger. But don't ever get turned on in a session with me. And the highest insult you could ever inflict is to ask me to do anything for your sexual arousal.

Most massage practitioners simply go into this unconscious puritanical denial about human sexual nature. For me, I realized my comfort zone did not include being in a role as erotic masseur for anyone at anytime. What I did clearly want to do,

though, was to teach others how to nurture and pleasure their friends and lovers both sexually and nonsexually—massage had opened so many meaningful avenues for me both in lovemaking and in friendships.

So I invited several of my friends and lovers to explore, share, and develop massage strokes for the genitals. In a few months I sent out a flyer for my first Erotic Massage for Couples weekend seminar. It filled up quickly. Then the week just before the seminar, about half the couples developed cold feet and canceled. This was the San Francisco Bay Area, but a class in massage including the genital area was still a major psychological stretch for the most modern of modern lovers.

I too had many fears sailing into this uncharted arts-of-love-and-sex ocean. What if everyone freaks out and doesn't come back the second day? What if the seminar becomes an orgy—which in and of itself would be okay, but was clearly not my intent for the weekend? What if a partner of one couple makes a pass at a partner of another couple and a brawl erupts?

I wanted to teach massage strokes for the whole body, including the genitals. The relaxation of a foot bathing, the nurturing of a facial massage—these experiences could also occur with a genital massage.

Unlike the heated rush of my first intercourse on the Pennsylvania farmhouse plank floor, I wanted to teach how to be a lover with a slow hand. So I instructed with the Masters and Johnson approach of non-performance-nondemand.

Late Sunday afternoon at the completion of the first Erotic Massage seminar, we

M: A kitchen counter can serve equally well as a post.

F: Intense and animalistic. A great way to tease a man: bend over without any panties.

F: I get full penetration and his balls rub against my clitoris. When he pumps me faster, they stimulate my clitoris even more.

F: A quickie; a perfect break from the grind of cooking and cleaning.

F: Feels better in the shower. And it's easy when slippery.

F: Tea for two. Yes!

F: Good lying down with a sheet over you when other people might walk in. P.S. Wear a skirt without panties.

F: Another good one for depth of penetration but still allows face-to-face interaction.

M: Good for my pregnant partner.

F: Controlling the speed and the rhythm, he can even easily slide his penis into my ass when it gets real hot.

M: This one I like for making love with a Rubenesque woman.

F: A man with good hands (like my sweetie) is such a turn-on. It just makes me want to suck till I can't stand the pleasure anymore!

M: Nice way to start; no way to stop.

M: For me, it's hard to focus on what I'm doing when I'm being pleasured at the same time.

F: One of my favorite safe-sex positions. Mutual masturbation—both partners can fully see the other's genitals and can stimulate them with their hands.

F: A great way to start to play. Using the fingers and the tongue to start things rolling.

M: Notice the head support; very beneficial.

F: Scratch mine and I'll scratch yours.

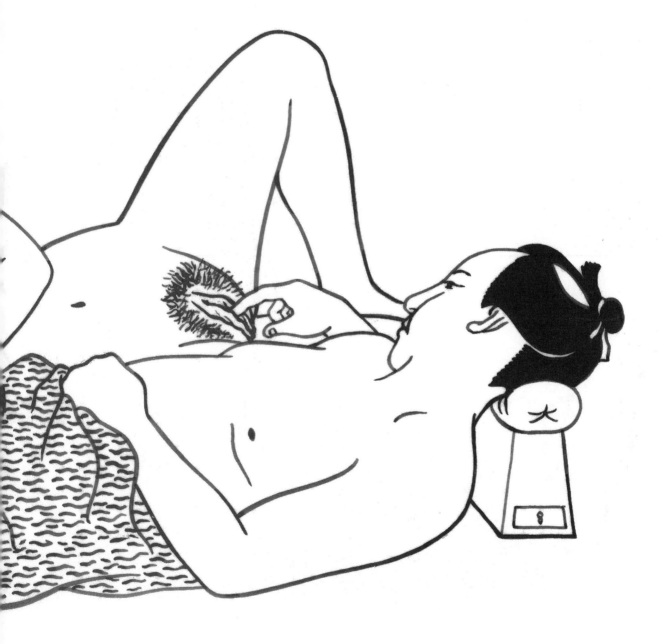

F: Come tell Santa what you want. . . .

F: A nice position when I'm feeling affectionate and sit on my lover's lap . . . and then things heat up and the clothes come off.

F: Good for a quickie in the bathroom while on the toilet. A midday delight!

F: This is easy for me because I've got long legs. Again the right height chair and a strong partner to lift me up slightly creates a relaxing screwing plus I can rub my clit or my partner can.

M: Do this one in front of big mirrors.

F: The wake-up call: one of those early a.m., not-quite-awake-yet cuddlies.

F: Made me very animalistic and submissive.

M: Wonderfully intimate. I prefer placing one of my hands on my partner's heart chakra as well.

F: Allows for G-spot arousal.

discovered land without falling off the ends of the Earth. My personal vision of how massage and sexuality could blend in harmony was now a reality.

In the next couple of years, I taught variations on this seminar to couples and individuals of all sexual lifestyles and orientations around the country. I was a missionary of sorts, preaching a different vision of the sacred and the sexual, sometimes labeling the instruction as tantric massage for meditators, sometimes as sensate therapy for professionals.

In the seminar, I would ask for a volunteer from the participants for the next set of massage strokes. Sometime in the first year, as I became more aware of the subtleties in the seminar, I realized that after the genital massage demonstration, the female or male volunteer would be in somewhat of a daze.

For most, when the genitals are touched in a pleasurable manner, orgasm becomes the usual anticipation. Since this was not my focus, I very consciously role-modeled a nonorgasmic approach in the instruction. The massage, however, was far from a sterile, clinical technique. I wanted the participants to realize in their bodies a deeper, more profound means of discovering the senses. When I noticed the volunteer might be coming close to the point of no return, I would change the stroke, the pressure, the area of concentration, perhaps remind the recipient to allow the breath to flow more easily, more fully, so she or he could feel the sexual energy building.

After I finished demonstrating the series of strokes, I would invite the volunteer to slowly return to his or her practice area in the room. This is when I would notice the spacy gaze, the awkward movement, more so than after a usual relaxing massage.

As a meditator might say, the snake was biting the brain. All that built-up energy had overintensified in one area. So the everyday mind was spinning its wheels. In this case, the energy was mostly sexual arousal, and the orgasm was not there as an explosive dispersion.

Then, partly by accident, partly by intuition, and partly by theory, I discovered a way to expand the built-up arousal, to balance the energy throughout the recipient's body.

The method is simple. After the usual series of strokes on the genital area, I gently place one of my hands on the recipient's pelvic floor, with my palm cupping the vulva or the scrotum and penis. My other hand is on the top of the recipient's head (exactly as in the illustration on page 33).

Then I invite the recipient to inhale and imagine the breath entering at the pelvic floor, where one of my hands is touching. Continuing with the inhalation, the recipient is to both imagine and feel the breath as a flow of energy, a flow of awareness up the core of his or her body to the top of the head, where my other hand is touching. Then on the exhalation, the awareness flow is to be imagined and felt moving back down the core to the pelvic floor. This is repeated for a couple of minutes.

Complementing the recipient's pattern, I synchronize my inhalation and exhalation to the recipient's. For the breath and energy flowing up and down the recipient, I am *intending* that my energy assist the upward and downward flow. (This latter aspect may sound rather abstract and is probably not essential to the process.)

"Energized as well as very calm and relaxed" almost always was the volunteer's report after this "laying on of hands." Rarely did anyone say an orgasm was still needed to feel "complete." Rather than dazed, the volunteer often would appear centered. Even after hundreds of erotic massage instructions over fifteen years throughout North America and Europe, the response was usually the same.

The method is nothing profound. The process is already naturally within us, all of us.

What is profound is that I was willing to touch the genitals and dance with the sexual energy when it was appropriate and mutually consenting. Unfortunately, as long as the massage and other healing professions consider such practices abhorrent or inherently unethical, they will never discover the incredible transformative and healing possibilities that sexual energy can teach us.

In an erotic massage instruction, my role is as a compassionate facilitator rather than a lover. While not being insensitive to my own pleasure, the focus is on the recipient's flow.

Moreover, this particular sexual laying-on-of-hands process is very much a group experience. (The method is often less effective in a one-to-one situation.) With the other participants bringing so much focused attention to the demonstration, I and the recipient are drawing on a greatly intensified energetic field, probably very similar to

the ancient lovers' *hieros gamos*, or sacred marriage ceremony.

While this erotic massage technique fits easily into Tantric, Taoist, and Quodoushka theory, the style seems very close to the descriptions of karezza I was to read a few years later. Variations on a method such as my rediscovery seem to have been more common with ancient lovers who were also familiar with meditation and the subtle aspects of sexual energy.

For me, though, discovering the technique was practically a quantum leap. I shifted from abstract theory to personal embodiment. Transforming sexual energy was no longer a concept I labored to comprehend from weathered texts. Once I realized I could repeat the experience for myself and others, deep inside I knew a world of knowledge was awaiting my continued awakening to it.

Experience, not dogma, had become my teacher.

❦

When I had headed out on the hippie trip across North America with Shannon, I thought I was leaving academia behind for good. Once single again and settled in San Francisco, though, I found myself taking seminars and classes at a variety of universities, colleges, and institutes in the university of life, as I called the Bay Area. By then, Human Sexuality 101 had become a common course. So I decided to take it at the local community college just a mile down the road.

Before Masters and Johnson's *Human Sexual Response* (1966) and *Human Sexual Inadequacy* (1970), academic courses based

F: Great position for foreplay to start out hugging with kissing and caressing . . . and then when we're both hot, sliding my lover's cock inside of me. It usually ends up with him lying down and me on top straddling.

M: It's so warm and wet; I can feel everything.

F: Do it on a firm surface. Like it because my lover and I are very close: chest to chest, nose to nose. Plus my lover can stimulate my asshole and grab my cheeks, which I love.

F: Builds strong bodies and feels good too!

F: Good control for woman—the up and down action feels wonderful.

M: Works better for me when the woman has cushions under her buttocks.

M: We ended up in this position when the woman was having lubrication problems, and this solved it.

F: Bow wow! RRRRRFFFF!! I feel like a dog or cat and insist my partner bite me on the back of my neck and ears.

F: Great for G-spot stimulation. Like it when my partner rubs my clit here.

F: Our regular favorite (top 10).

M: The erotic view is too much.

F: This little piggy went to the market. This little piggy stayed at home. This little piggy went wee wee—all the way home.

F: I usually sleep in the fetal position, and my lover would crawl up behind me and just slide in.

F: Believe it or not, this is EXCELLENT for when I have menstrual cramps!

F: Many of these drawings emphasize the penis. However, as a lesbian, I can attest to the fact that they work ever so nicely woman to woman. We simply focus on other things.

F: Being under the covers on a good cold winter night, a great way to warm up!

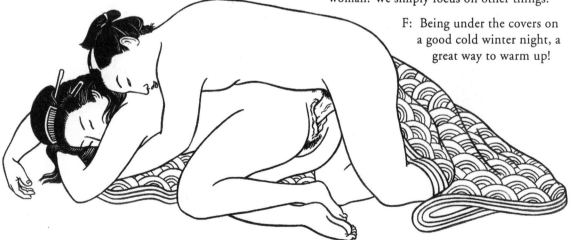

F: Sex in a Jacuzzi is very steamy. Love the weightless feeling.

F: We don't have a hot tub, so we couldn't do this one though I love the idea and the woman's ecstatic image.

M: What else do you do in a hot tub?

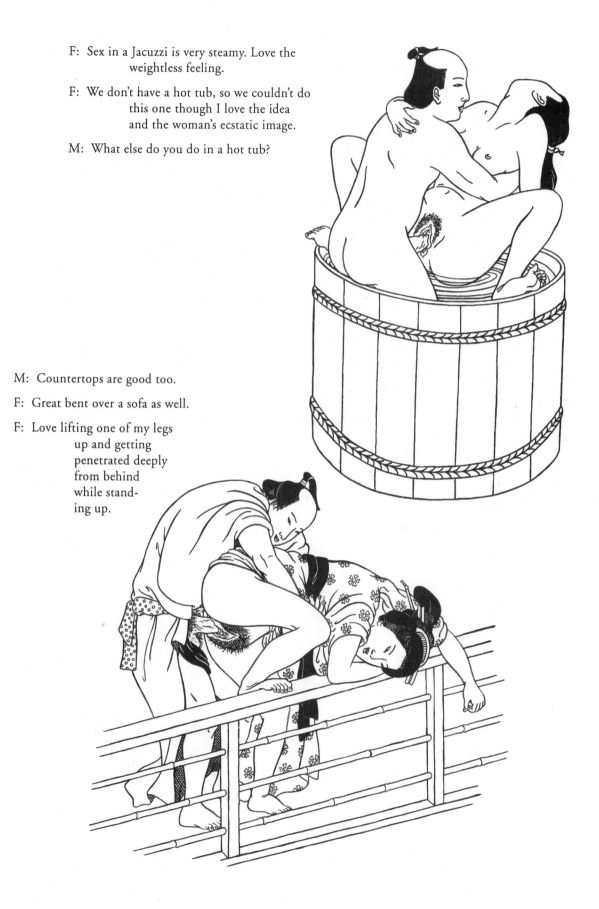

M: Countertops are good too.

F: Great bent over a sofa as well.

F: Love lifting one of my legs up and getting penetrated deeply from behind while stand-ing up.

F: Sex *is* the great outdoors.

F: Especially in a park where there are people around and
   you can be discovered.

F: Sex in nature is always magical for me, something raw
   and pure to lie down on the grass and make
   love. Though it doesn't hurt to have a blanket.

F: Going on a hike and then seducing your lover and
   pulling him into the bushes is a great thrill.

F: Does it count in a football stadium?

F: A great way to cuddle and talk about the day.

F: Easy, gentle rocking together sure feels fine.

F: Here we eye gaze and align our
      chakras, especially opening
      the heart, the third eye,
      and the sexual
      centers.

F: But Honey, I was trying to get a suntan.

M: Table height is crucial or you'll kill your back.

F: My man finds it highly erotic to watch us and
      himself.

M: Kitchen counters will work for this also.

F: Works on a Pouf/Ottoman too!

entirely on an interdisciplinary approach to sexuality were basically unheard of. Two decades earlier, Kinsey's earthquakes, *Sexual Behavior in the Human Male* (1948) and *Sexual Behavior in the Human Female* (1953), had severely cracked the sex-is-sin infrastructure. But not until Masters and Johnson's books, *the pill*, and the massive countercultural movement of the late 1960s were the puritan prison's gates blasted wide open for the modern lover in America.

Because of my academic background and my erotic massage course, I was invited to teach a course on body approaches in sex therapy and sex education at the Institute for the Advanced Study of Human Sexuality, a graduate school in San Francisco.

While by that time I had taken a couple more classes in human sexuality, I felt if I were to train future sex therapists and sex educators, I had better learn a great deal more about Western sexology. So I began taking courses at the institute, which happened to be one of the few places in the world one could pursue a graduate degree specifically in human sexuality.

Sexology as an established scientific endeavor had really begun shortly after the turn of this century, principally in Germany. On May 6, 1933, a Nazi mob quickly brought a significant halt to many of those early developments by ransacking the prestigious Institute for Sexology in Berlin.

This was only three months after Hitler had came to power. Publicly burning the Berlin institute's books and papers, the Nazis were conveniently eliminating the records of some prominent Nazis who had been patients at the institute's clinic. (There has also been speculation that some records

were actually confiscated by the Nazis in order to blackmail people in positions of power.)

By the mid-1970s when I began to teach and study at the institute in San Francisco, sexology again was in an innovative period of new research and new conceptual frameworks. Since the institute was continuously bringing in prominent sex researchers, therapists, and educators to lecture, I was able to feel the vibrancy of a scholarly rebirth and many of the innovators behind it.

My main interests then, however, could have been labeled *erotology* more than *sexology*. The latter term is defined as the interdisciplinary, scientific study of sexuality (*scientia sexualis*). Over the ages, many fears and false beliefs about sexual functioning and lifestyles have pervaded. Modern research methods clearly have brought much more light to bear on the negative influences of the Dark Ages.

Erotology focuses on the practical aspects of lovemaking (*ars amatoria*). How can I be a better lover? What are the most effective techniques when I wish to pleasure another or myself? Erotic massage is one set of techniques amongst many possibilities, as suggested in both ancient and modern how-to amatory books.

The conceptual distinction between erotology and sexology in many ways is superficial and academic. Clearly, though, the scientific approach of sexology is what has enabled the relegitimization of sex in the Western world. Unfortunately, professional sexual practices are legitimate only if they can be deemed as sex *therapy* or sex *education*. Professional sexual *pleasure*, however, often still remains condemned as unethical, illegitimate, or illegal at worst, and hedonistic at best.

At the same time I was teaching and studying sexuality at the institute, I was also often deeply involved in meditation with a Tibetan Buddhist lama. He spoke of sex only once in the several years I sat cross-legged in his lecture-meditation room. How to meditate in a way to more deeply experience the subtle energies in and around our bodies was my main learning from that ancient tradition, sometimes referred to as Tantric Buddhism. (*Tantra* here is used in a far broader sense than the contemporary *tantric sexuality* term.)

Rinpoche, a common respectful title for a lama, taught that meditation is not the activity a meditator does, especially not the physical form. Rather, meditation is the mindful awareness a person brings to an activity or situation. A meditation practice can indeed facilitate developing the mindfulness, but the practice is not meditation in itself.

The distinction between the activity and the mindfulness is essential if we are to comprehend that sex can be meditation. Most of us do our principal spiritual activities in a religious context, maybe in a church, synagogue, temple, or ashram, perhaps around an established altar. Given that most contemporary religious dogmas prohibit sexual expression in these contexts, it would indeed be a major shift to hold sex as spiritual.

Adapting the mindfulness approach to my sexual activities (as well as any other activity in life), I was able to add meditation to my lovemaking. Moreover, I could never have taught erotic massage effectively if I had not brought a very mindful attentiveness to the recipient's response, my own feelings, my touch, my words while teaching, and the energetic dynamics of the other participants observing the presentation.

Integrating Rinpoche's teachings with what I was learning from Dr. Chang, erotic massage teaching, and Western sexology was leading me into both a wise old world and a brave new world outside the oppressive sex-negative mold of 4,000 years.

❦

Then I met SwiftDeer.

Raised on a Texas farm by his Cherokee mother and Irish father, SwiftDeer often likes to describe himself as a cowboy who'd rather be riding brahma bulls, and as a former Marine. Recently, he was also elected to the World Martial Arts Hall of Fame.

He is another skillful bicultural messenger, drawing principally from his Native American traditions. After many years of training and preparation, SwiftDeer now sits on the Council of Elders of the Twisted Hairs Metis Medicine Society. *Metis* means mixed, and *twisted hairs* refers to selecting powerful teachings from many different traditions and bringing them into an integrated, beautiful braid. This particular intertribal council of shamans and medicine women and men from North, Central, and South America has been functioning since the early 1200s C.E.

A masterful storyteller, SwiftDeer often reminds us to never believe anything he says. "You must experience the truth for yourself." His intent as a teacher clearly is to support an individual in being a warrior—a

M: An erotic turn-on.

F: Takes a lot of physical doing.

F: I think the secret here is propping on pillows properly, or maybe doing yoga from age five, but I never achieved that swanlike sweep.

F: Okay, this one I've never done. I'm going to make it a point to try it though. One problem: the woman has to support all of her weight on her arms, but then again being upside down can really be a head rush.

F: This only worked for me with my elbows bent. Couldn't stay there long enough!

F: Heads or tails?

warrior whose battle is with his or her own limitations.

This is the context in which I came to take an introductory Quodoushka weekend seminar in northern California with SwiftDeer, his partner NightBird, and several of his apprentices.

First, we began Friday evening with the talking stick. When an individual holds this staff from the plant world, often embellished with elements from the mineral and animal worlds, individuals are to give the speaker their full attention without interruption. Talking and listening is brought into a ceremonial circle.

Sexual abuse had become a popular societal issue at that time. So SwiftDeer asked us each to share how we had been sexually abused. The seminar had about fifty participants, and my turn to hold the talking stick did not come around the circle until the next morning.

I had all night to ponder the question. Sexual abuse—I just couldn't think of events where that concept applied to me. Yes, I had had some uncomfortable sexual experiences in my childhood. These were a part of the common trial-and-error, growing-up experiences. Yes, one or maybe a couple of adults from both genders had made unpreferred, subtle advances when I was a teenager. But so what? There was no coercion, and the infringements were very minor compared to the many nonsexual authority games some adults perpetrated. If, however, I had ever received an invitation from one of my fantasies, I bet I would have gladly consented, regardless of age differences. I wonder what ever happened to that tenth grade Latin teacher. . . .

Then my answer to SwiftDeer's question hit me like a ton of bricks. No specific person had ever sexually abused me. But my religious and general culture had imposed deep in my psyche a fucking lie: Sex is sinful, inherently so, except maybe within very narrow parameters.

I was in rage. I realized I had unconsciously bought the belief. As a child, I had accepted sex-is-sin as part of my self-definition. Many years now had been spent finding my way out of that repressed cave.

A very simple ceremony had brought forth the compelling realization. While the idea in the recognition was nothing new or profound, the profundity came in the process of the "ah ha"—a result more likely within a ceremonial context than in usual intellectual analysis.

The talking stick ceremony was only the introduction. Next, NightBird opened the teachings with the sacred pipe ceremony. Here she honored Great Spirit, Grandmother Earth, Grandfather Sun, the four directions, the plant, mineral, animal, and human worlds, and more of what blesses and sustains us in our daily lives.

The remainder of the weekend was primarily devoted to exercises, or meditations as I call them, to open our awareness to our senses, our physical body, and our subtle energetic bodies. Some of the perspectives were similar to what I had studied in Taoism and Tantra. This was of no surprise. Physical and energetic anatomy is basically the same regardless of whether our increasingly mixed genetic pools derive primarily from Asia, Africa, Europe, Turtle Island, or elsewhere.

F: Does doing it on a Harley-Davidson count?

F: Never done this, but boy, have I fantasized about it. Can anyone help me out?

F: Just riding a horse by myself can be quite sensual—the movement of the horse, the smell and feel of the leather saddle. . . .

M: Makes for some great motion!

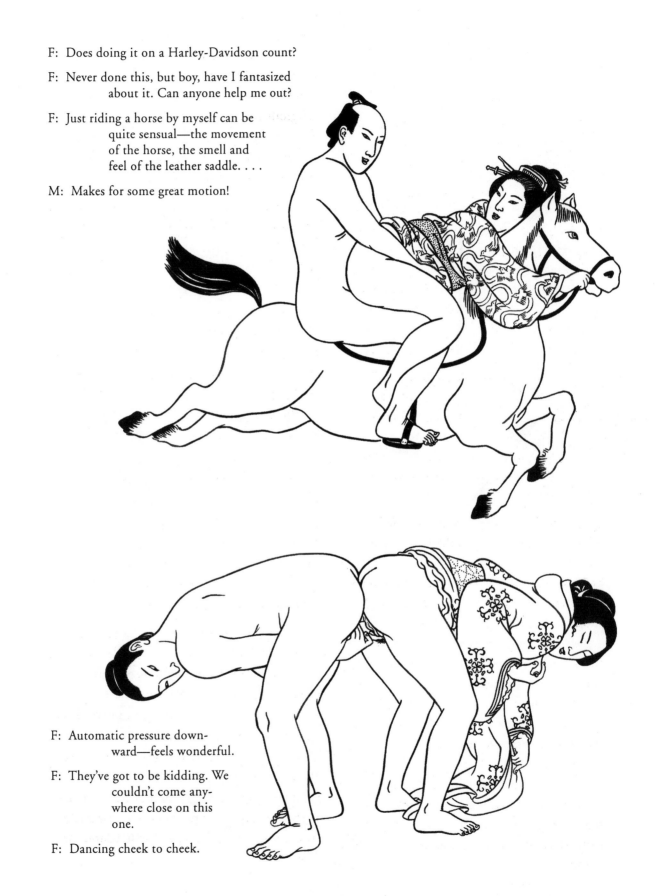

F: Automatic pressure downward—feels wonderful.

F: They've got to be kidding. We couldn't come anywhere close on this one.

F: Dancing cheek to cheek.

F: Wet dreams!

F: The BEST bath I ever had.

M: We used a boogie board in
     the pool and had a ball.

F: An ultimate sexual high. Very relaxing to just drift in the water and have your lover lick you to climax. Heaven on Earth or damn close to it!

F: Ethereal—lying on my back in the water and getting my pussy licked.

For me at least, SwiftDeer was saving the blast for last. The FireBreath Orgasm, as the meditation is often called, is usually a combination of muscular contractions and releases, an intense breathing pattern, a pelvic movement pattern, and an awareness process of connecting various subtle energetic centers often referred to as chakras along the core of the body.

The meditation can be done with or without a partner, with or without sexual stimulation. Over time, the technique can be developed and modified so one can even do the meditation in public without being noticed.

Lying on a pad on the floor, NightBird began to demonstrate the technique while SwiftDeer described the specific actions. When you inhale, you contract certain muscles this way. Then when you exhale, you push those muscles that way. . . . Next you add a pelvic rotation this way when you inhale and that way when you exhale. . . . Now imagine and feel the energy move from one chakra to the next chakra as you inhale and exhale. . . .

Then SwiftDeer said, "Okay, everyone, let's do it. That's how you learn it."

By now I was thoroughly confused. I wandered back to my practice area on the floor, wondering how I could possibly pat my head, rub my stomach in a counterclockwise direction, chew gum, and recite the Gettysburg address silently—all at once in a specific sequence. It was sort of comical, though I wasn't laughing.

I lay down on my back, still confused, closed my eyes, and began to try to put together this FireBreath Orgasm puzzle I had

heard so much about. Meanwhile, in the background SwiftDeer's apprentices began burning in a conch shell several dried herbs commonly used in ceremonies: sage, lavender, and sweetgrass.

From time to time SwiftDeer would call out reminders of the technique or other suggestions. I could also hear others around the room breathing forcefully and occasionally releasing intense vocal sounds that sure sounded like something associated with at least some type of orgasm. "How come it's so easy for everyone else?" I thought to myself, beating myself up for not remembering the sequence.

Perhaps fifteen or thirty minutes into the practice—I had no idea of the time—I heard NightBird close beside my ear. An excellent ceremony leader who knows how to use different vocal qualities to support different intents, she calmly offered me words of encouragement. Then I felt her fan me with a bird's wing. She was smudging my energetic field with the herbal smoke from a conch shell.

NightBird's presence eased my frustrations.

Trying to remember all the combinations and permutations though, I soon found my impatience returning. Then when I thought SwiftDeer might be bringing the practice session to a close, I said to myself, "Last chance. Just breathe and fuckin' do it, Ray."

I shifted my awareness to breathing deeper and more intensely. "Feel the energy," I instructed myself. My mind seemed to let go of what-to-do-when. "The techniques are not really what's important now."

Suddenly there was no sound, no movement, nothing.

Then I became conscious of what felt like my legs, pelvis, and part of my back up in the air. My shoulders and head were firmly on the floor. None of this was really clear except that I now again had a bodily consciousness. I had no idea where I had gone. I knew only I was now back.

Shortly afterward, as I lay breathing on the floor, no longer doing the techniques, I felt subtle, pleasurable vibrations throughout my body. I was calm, peaceful, in some ways similar to after a sexual orgasm. Lingering in the glow, I sensed I had taken a quantum leap.

There had been no genital stimulation, no ejaculation. As far as I could tell, there had been no rhythmic pelvic floor muscular contractions, which are a standard criterion in a Masters and Johnson definition of a sexual orgasm. Moreover, I had never felt sexual in the exercise.

Yet, the only word I could use to explain my mind-eliminating experience was *orgasm.*

I had come to the ancient Quodoushka world to learn more. The experience I had in the FireBreath Orgasm practice, though, is no more "ancient" than "modern." The experience is inherently within each of us, potentially accessible by all.[17]

I have been fortunate in finding several ancient lover teachers in my personal and professional quest. In varying ways, these teachers have all taught the value of mental, physical, emotional, spiritual, and sexual harmony.

Live teachers, however, are not as accessible as the increasing number of texts from ancient lovers and adaptations from ancient lovers by modern lovers. *Secret Sexual Positions* is such an introductory adaptation.

The sexual position—with its myriad variations—is a powerful symbol of our human sexual nature. Embracing the spiritual beauty of the body and the sexual connection is an ancient lovers' expression we as modern lovers can continue to discover.

This has been my intent in sharing here my interweaving of ancient and modern lovers' strands into a beautiful braid.

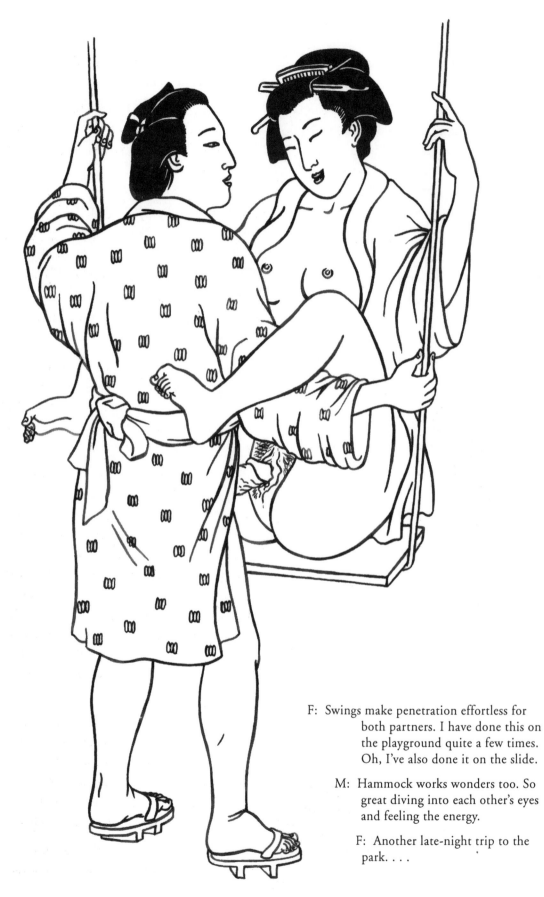

F: Swings make penetration effortless for both partners. I have done this on the playground quite a few times. Oh, I've also done it on the slide.

M: Hammock works wonders too. So great diving into each other's eyes and feeling the energy.

F: Another late-night trip to the park. . . .

The Secrets

So what is so secret about the sexual positions in this book?

Nothing really, unless we lack access to the information. And most of the world has lacked this access until the last half century or so.

Books like the *Kama Sutra*, *Ananga-Ranga*, and *Ishimpo* were for the elite: the royalty, the wealthy, the intelligentsia, and in some cases principally the male gender. Usually the masses lacked the money to obtain, the education to comprehend, and perhaps the cultural approval to have such writings.

Knowledge is power. In Chinese writings, the texts on sexual techniques promoting longevity sometimes appeared as coveted possessions that the Emperor would lock away in secret vaults.

Controlling information access is also a common societal control method. Train the masses to believe that something as innately pervasive as sexual desire and sexual action are sinful. Add absolution of the sin is possible only through representatives of the religious dogma. Add a donation prerequisite, a fine, or a penalty for absolution. Add censorship to prevent alternative views and information. The result is one of the most effective means of social control ever devised.

The modern lover entering the twenty-first century, in contrast, has unprecedented opportunities to learn more about the profoundness of our sexual nature. New sexual information and ancient sexual wisdom are increasingly at our fingertips.

My life's journey has taken me into several ancient and modern lovers' worlds.

From these experiences, I have gleaned from others or discovered on my own several secrets.

More accurately, they are my points of view about sexuality becoming a more meaningful, a more joyful experience and expression in our lives.

First, the main secret about sexual positions is that for most of us most of the time, sexual positions are the least important aspect of lovemaking.

Not for all of us all of the time, though. At least occasional variation in any habitual behavior can release new awarenesses and appreciations. Additionally, for a myriad of reasons including anatomical compatibility, a different sexual position can sometimes indeed make a world of difference for a particular partner in terms of sexual satisfaction or healing an illness (as in the Taoist view).

Second, while taboo sex is often secretive sex, if taboo sex is as good as it gets, we're missing the boat. This is not referring to what the general culture defines as taboo sex. Indeed, where sex is sin, most forms of sex are culturally taboo. What is *personally* taboo sex is the point here.

If in the pulpit we preach sex is sinful, but later in the week at a motel we get our rocks off by watching a clandestine connection pull down her underwear. . . . We might call it the TV Evangelist Syndrome. Watching such a clandestine sexual connection can be a mutually joyful exchange. However, believing and feeling the event is evil are what make the action a perversion.

Forbidden for occasional adventure can be fun. If it has to feel forbidden on an ongoing basis in order to be sexually gratifying, we are greatly limiting one of the most profound aspects of being a human being.

Third, honesty and communication are essential for truly satisfying sex, regardless if it's a one-night encounter or a long-term connection. Withholding the truth or blatant misrepresentation robs the emotional and energetic flows that are integral parts of sexual exchange.

Being honest and communicating it may be difficult in many situations. In the long run, though, the benefits far outweigh the disadvantages.

Communicating our truth honors the other.

Fourth, the most useful skill a lover can learn is nurturing, sensual massage. (Often the approaches in therapeutic or athletic styles of massage are too mechanical or rough.)

In teaching erotic and sexual methods to both sexology professionals and nonprofessionals, I have always felt that sensitive, aware touch is the single, most valuable tool in the arts of love and sex. Refinement of abilities with taste, smell, sound, and sight are indeed important arts as well, but touch and massage seem to be primary.

Finally, developing a meditation practice is probably the most effective way to become a more skillful and compassionate lover in general. If the meditation method emphasizes sensory awareness, the abilities are likely to be even more easily transferable to lovemaking.

Bringing a mindful awareness to our sensual-sexual dance can enhance the aliveness of what we give to another and how we receive from another.

❦

These are my sexual secrets.

They are summed up in a prayer I learned from SwiftDeer, who had learned it from Grandfather Two Bears.[18]

The *Navaho Blessed BeautyWay Prayer*, while not about sexuality specifically nor from the Quodoushka path, conveys the essence of being a wise lover, either ancient or modern.

Here *beauty* is integrity, compassion, harmony, balance, an open heart guided by discernment.

Walking in beauty with our sexuality is no simple task. We must make it our conscious intent.

Sex is good.

Sex is holy.

Celebrate it!

Great Spirit, may we walk in Beauty.

May Beauty be above us so that we dream of Beauty.

May Beauty be in front of us so that we are led by Beauty.

May Beauty be to the left of us so that we may receive Beauty.

May Beauty be to the right of us so that we may give out Beauty.

May Beauty be behind us so that those who come after us may see Beauty.

May Beauty be inside us so that we might become Beauty.

Great Spirit, may we walk in Beauty.

F: I don't play the guitar, but I wonder if it would matter anyway.

M: For the musically inclined with good multiple-attention skills.

F: This would take a lot of talent . . . and balance.

F: A-pickin' and a-grinnin'.

Selected Positions

from the

Kama Sutra

by

Vatsyayana

Most descriptions indicating the male being in charge of all the actions are edited so that the female is now more of an equal participant and initiator.

An ingenious person should multiply the kinds of congress after the fashion of the different kinds of beasts and of birds. For these different kinds of congress, performed according to the . . . liking of each individual, generate love, friendship, and respect in the hearts of women.
(p. 109)

Widely opened position
    When she lowers her head and raises her middle parts.

Yawning position
    When she raises her thighs and keeps them wide apart.

Position of Indrani
    When she places her thighs with her legs doubled on them upon her sides.

Clasping position
    When the legs of both the male and the female are stretched straight out over each other. It is of two kinds, the side position and the supine position.

Pressing position
    When, after congress has begun in the clasping position, the woman presses her lover with her thighs.

Twining position
    When the woman places one of her thighs across the thigh of her lover.

Mare's position
    When a woman forcibly holds in her yoni the lingam after it is in.

Rising position

When the female raises both of her thighs straight up.

Yawning position

When she raises both of her legs, and places them on her lover's shoulder.

Pressed position

When the legs are contracted, and thus held by the lover before his bosom.

Half-pressed position

When only one of her legs is stretched out.

Splitting of a bamboo position

When the woman places one of her legs on her lover's shoulder, and stretches the other out, and then places the latter on his shoulder, and stretches out the other, and continues to do so alternately.

Fixing of a nail

When one of her legs is placed on the head, and the other is stretched out.

Crab's position

When both the legs of the woman are contracted and placed on her stomach.

Packed position

When the thighs are raised and placed one upon the other.

Lotuslike position

When the shanks are placed one upon the other.

Turning position

When a man, during congress, turns round, and enjoys the woman without leaving her, while she embraces him round the back all the time.

Supported congress

When a man and a woman support themselves on each other's bodies, or on a wall, or pillar, and thus while standing.

Suspended congress

When a man supports himself against a wall, and the woman, sitting on his hands joined together and held underneath her, throws her arms round his neck, and putting her thighs alongside his waist, moves herself by her feet, which are touching the wall against which the man is leaning.

Congress of a cow

When a woman stands on her hands and feet like a quadruped, and her lover mounts her like a bull. At this time everything that is ordinarily done on the bosom should be done on the back.

United congress

When a man enjoys two women at the same time, both of whom love him equally.

Lower congress

When congress is in the anus.

Selected Positions

from the

Perfumed Garden

by

Sheikh Nefzawi

Most descriptions indicating the male being in charge of all the actions are edited so that the female is now more of an equal participant and initiator.

Brackets indicate a significant modification of content or terms.

First posture

The woman lies on her back and raises her thighs; then, getting between her legs, the man introduces his member. Gripping the ground with his toes, he will be able to move in a suitable manner. This posture is a good one for males who have long members.

Second Posture

If the male's member is short, the woman lies on her back and he raises her legs in the air so that her toes touch her ears. Her buttocks being thus raised, the vulva is thrown forward. Now he introduces his member.

Third posture

She lies on the ground and he gets between her thighs; then, with one of her legs on his shoulder and the other under his arm, he penetrates her.

Fourth posture

She stretches on the ground and puts her legs on his shoulders; in that position his member will be exactly opposite her vulva which will be lifted off the ground. That is the moment he introduces his member.

Fifth posture

The woman lies on her side on the ground; then, lying down and getting between her thighs, the man introduces his member. This posture is apt to give rise to rheumatic or sciatic pains.

Sixth posture

The woman rests on her knees and elbows in the position for prayer. In this posture the vulva stands out behind. He enters her thus.

Seventh posture

The woman is on her side; then the male, sitting on his heels, will place her top leg on his nearest shoulder and her other leg against his thighs. She will keep on her side, and he will be between her legs. He introduces his member and moves her backwards and forwards with his hands.

Eighth posture

With the woman on her back, he kneels astride her.

Ninth posture

The woman rests, either face forward or the reverse, against a slightly raised platform, her feet remaining on the ground and her body projecting in front. She will thus present her vulva to the man's member, which he will introduce.

Tenth posture

The woman is on a rather low divan, grasping the woodwork with her hands; then with her legs on his hips and gripping his body, he will introduce his member, at the same time grasping the divan. When the lovers begin to work, they let their movements keep time.

Eleventh posture

The woman lies on her back with her buttocks raised by a cushion placed under them. She puts the soles of her feet together with the man between her thighs.

The closure

The woman lies on her back, her buttocks raised with a cushion; then the man gets between her legs, keeping his toes on the floor, and presses her thighs against her chest. Now he passes his hands under her arms to clasp her to himself, or tightly grips her shoulders. That done, he introduces his member and draws her towards himself at the moment of ejaculation. This posture may be painful for the woman, for, with her thighs pressed on her chest and her buttocks raised with the cushion, the walls of the vagina are forced together, and, as a consequence—the uterus being pushed forward—there is not enough room for the penis which can only be inserted with difficulty, and which impinges on the womb. This posture should only be used when the penis is short and soft.

The frog's posture

The woman is on her back and her thighs raised till her heels are close to her buttocks. Now the man seats himself in front of her vulva and introduces his member; then putting her knees under his armpits and, grasping the upper part of her arms, he draws her to himself at the propitious moment.

The clasping of hands and feet

With the woman on her back, the man sits on his heels between her thighs and grips the floor with his toes; she will now put her legs round his body and he will put his arms about her neck.

The raised legs posture

While the woman is lying on her back, the man takes hold of her legs and, holding them close together, raises them until her soles point to the ceiling; then clasping her between his thighs, he introduces his member, taking care at the same time not to let her legs fall.

The goat's posture

The woman lies on her side and stretches out the bottom leg. The man crouches down between her thighs, lifts her top leg and intro-

F: So *this* is the Wheelbarrow Polka.

F: This can be good if your lover is about
    the same height you are, with
    good, strong arms.

F: A moment's distraction left me with
    a bumped head and bad
    humor—not conducive
    to ecstatic lovemaking.

M: Another erotic view.

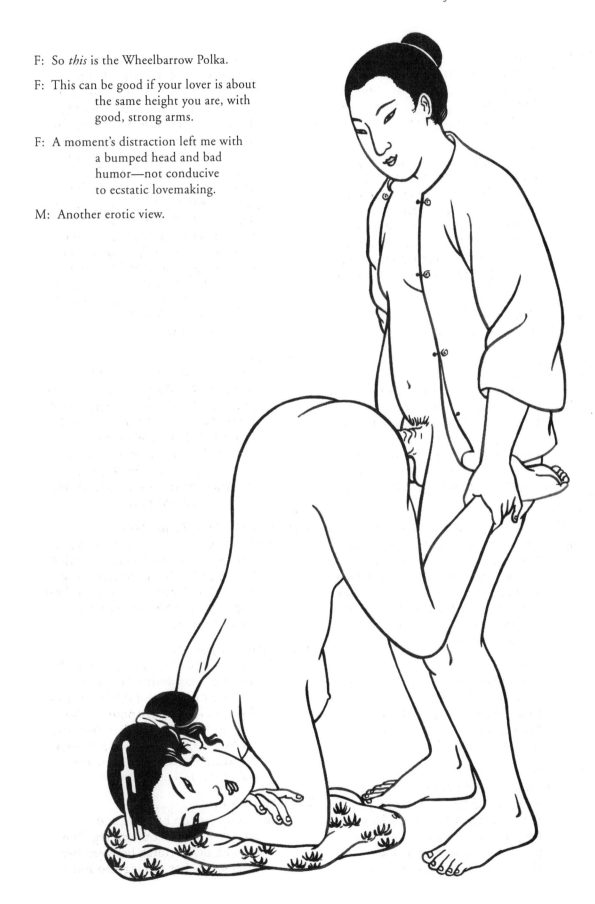

duces his member. He holds her by the arms or shoulders.

The Archimedean screw

While the man is lying on his back, the woman sits on his member, keeping her face towards his. She then places her hands on the bed, at the same time keeping her belly off his; she now moves up and down and, if the man is light in weight, he may move as well. If the woman wishes to kiss the man, she need only lay her arms on the bed.

[The ancient swing]

The woman is suspended face upwards from the ceiling by means of four cords [wide sashes] attached to her hands and feet and another supporting the middle of her body. Her position should be such that her vulva is now opposite his member, the man standing up. He introduces his member and then begins to swing her, first away from him, then towards him. He thus alternately introduces and withdraws his member, and so he continues until he ejaculates.

The somersault

The woman should let her trousers fall to her ankles so that they are like fetters. She then bends down till her head is in her trousers, when the man, holding her legs, pulls her over onto her back. He then kneels down and penetrates her. It is said that there are women, who, when lying on their back, can put their feet under their head without the help of their hands or trousers.

The ostrich's tail

The women lies on the ground and kneels at her feet; then he raises her legs and places them round his neck so that only her head and shoulders remain on the ground. Now he penetrates her.

Putting on the sock

The woman being on her back, the male sits between her legs and places his member between the lips of her vulva which he grasps with the thumb and first finger. He then moves so that the part of his member which is in contact with the woman is subjected to rubbing, and continues so until her vulva is moist with the liquid which escapes from his penis. Having thus given her a foretaste of pleasure, he enters her completely.

The mutual view of the buttocks

The man lies on his back, and the woman, turning her back to him, sits on his member. He now clasps her body with his legs and she leans over until her hands touch the floor. Thus supported she has a view of his buttocks, and he of hers, and she is able to move conveniently.

Drawing the bow

The woman lies on her side, and the man, also on his side, gets between her legs so that his face is turned towards her back; now, placing his hands on her shoulders, he introduces his member. The woman then grasps the man's feet and draws them towards her; she forms thus, with the man's body, a bow to which she is the arrow.

Reciprocating motion

The man, seated on the ground, brings the soles of his feet together, at the same time lowering his thighs. The woman then sits on his feet and clasps his body with her legs and his neck with her arms. The man then grasps the woman's legs, and, moving his feet towards his body, carries the woman within reach of his member, which he introduces. By a movement of his feet he now moves her backwards and forwards. The woman should take care to facilitate this movement by not pressing too heavily. If the man fears that his member will be

F: Oh, my partner LIKES the control he has with this one!

M: Can be rough on the man's inner thighs.

F: Impossible position for us, or I should say for me—
though we often do use a similar position for
eye gazing and opening our heart chakras.

drawn right out, he must grasp the woman round the body and be satisfied with such movement as he can give with his feet.

[Sitting on the member]

The man sits down and stretches out his legs, and the woman sits on his thighs and crosses her legs behind his back. She places her vulva opposite his penis and lends a guiding hand. She then puts her arms round his neck, and he puts his round her waist and raises and lowers her on his member, in which movement she assists.

Coition from behind

The woman lies face downwards and raises her buttocks with a cushion; the man lies on her back and introduces his member while she slips her arms through his elbows.

The sheep's posture

The woman kneels down and puts her forearms on the ground; the man kneels down behind her and slips his penis in her vulva, which she makes stand out as much as possible. His hands should be placed on her shoulders.

The camel's hump

The woman, who is standing, bends forward till her fingers touch the floor; the man gets behind and copulates, at the same time grasping her thighs. If the man withdraws while the woman is still bending down, the vagina emits a sound like the bleating of a calf, and for that reason some women object to the posture.

[Standing on the wall]

While facing each other, the woman, hanging with her arms round the man's neck, raises her legs and with them clasps him round the waist, resting her feet against a wall. The man now introduces his member.

The fusion of love

The woman lies on her right side and the man on his left; he stretches his bottom leg straight down and raises his other leg, letting it rest on the woman's side. Now he pulls the woman's top leg onto his body and then introduces his member. The woman may help if she likes, to make the necessary movements.

Inversion

The man lies on his back and the woman lies on him. She grasps his thighs and draws them towards her, thus bringing his member into prominence. Having guided it in, she puts her hands on the bed, one on each side of the man's buttocks. It is necessary for her feet to be raised on a cushion to allow for the slope of the penis. The woman moves. This posture may be varied by the woman sitting on her heels between the man's legs.

Riding the member

The man lies down and places a cushion under his shoulders, taking care that his buttocks remain on the floor. Thus placed, he raises his legs till his knees are close to his face. The woman then sits on his member. She does not lie down, but sits astride, as though on a saddle formed by the man's legs and chest. By bending her knees, she can now move upwards and downwards; or she may put her knees on the floor, in which case the man moves her with his thighs while she grasps his shoulders.

The jointer

The man and the woman sit down facing each other; the woman then puts her right thigh on the man's left thigh, and he puts his right thigh on her left one. The woman guides his member into her vagina and grasps the man's arms while he grasps hers. They now indulge

F: Excedrin headache #68.

M: Wonderful view!

F: A ballet dancer's delight.

F: She must be a circus performer!

in a seesaw motion, leaning backwards and forwards alternately, taking care that their movements are well timed.

The stay-at-home

The woman lies on her back, and the man, with cushions under his hands, lies on her. When the introduction has taken place, the woman raises her buttocks as far as possible from the bed, and the man accompanies her in the movement, taking care that his member is not withdrawn. The woman then drops her buttocks with short sharp jerks, and, although the two are not clasped together, the man should keep quite close to the woman. They continue this movement, but it is necessary that the man be light and the bed soft; otherwise, pain will be caused.

The blacksmith's posture

The woman lies on her back with a cushion under her buttocks. She now draws her knees onto her chest so that her vulva stands out like a sieve; she then guides in the member. The man now performs for a moment or two the conventional movements. He then withdraws his member and slips it between the women's thighs in imitation of the blacksmith who draws the hot iron from the fire and plunges it into cold water.

The seductive posture

The woman lies on her back and the man crouches between her legs, which he then puts under his arms or on his shoulders. He may hold her by the waist or the arms.

M: Favorite of favorites, love to look at her . . . breasts,
curves, shoulders; to feel, see wild-eyed passion.

F: Love being on top and encouraging my lover to play
with my nipples. I control most of the motion
and can cum when I want.

F: Great for access to clitoral stimulation and adjusting
the amount of penetration.

M: No strain on my back or neck, and I can use my leg
muscles to raise my pelvis to meet my lover.

F: Nice way to visit and catch up with the day.

M: Freedom of my hands. What a view!

M: Who is who; where do I begin; where do you begin; our sexuality has made us one.

F: Great body contact and nice on cold days.

F: Nurturing and a nice way to go to sleep.

F: Good for when doggy style wears you out.

M: Loved the arm-hand entwining, to feel my partner pulling my upper body into her. She likes the G-spot "idling."

Selected Positions

from the

Ananga-Ranga

by

Kalyana Malla

The use of the original translation's *husband* and *wife* remains though most descriptions indicating the male being in charge of all the actions are edited so that the female is now more of an equal participant and initiator.

Samapada-uttana-bandha
> With the wife upon her back, both legs raised and placed upon his shoulders, the husband sits close to her and enjoys her.

Nagara-uttana-bandha
> With the wife upon her back, the husband sits between her legs, raises them both, keeping them on the other side of his waist, and enjoys her.

Traivikrama-uttana-bandha
> When one of the wife's legs is left lying upon the bed or carpet, the other being placed upon the head of the husband, who supports himself upon both hands.

Vyomapada-uttana-bandha
> When the wife, lying upon her back, raises with her hands both legs, drawing them as far back as her hair; the husband then sitting close to her, places both hands upon her breasts and enjoys her.

Smarachakrasana or the Kama's wheel position
> A mode very much enjoyed by the voluptuary. In this form the husband sits between the legs of his wife, extends his arms on both sides of her as far as he can, and thus enjoys her.

Avidarita
> When the wife raises both her legs, so that they may touch the bosom of her husband, who, sitting between her thighs, embraces and enjoys her.

Saumya-bandha

Given by the old poets to a form of congress much in vogue amongst the artful students of the Kama Shastra. The wife lies supine, and the husband, as usual, sits; he places both hands under her back, closely embracing her, which she returns by tightly grasping his neck.

Jrimbhits-asana

The wife's body is in the form of a bow with little pillows or pads beneath her hips and head. The husband then raises the seat of pleasure and rises to it by kneeling upon a cushion. This is an admirable form of congress, and is greatly enjoyed by both.

Veshtita-asana

When the wife lies upon her back cross-legged, and raises her feet a little; this position is very well fitted for those burning with desire.

Venuvidarita

The wife, lying upon her back, places one leg upon her husband's shoulder, and the other on the bed or carpet.

Sphutma-uttana-bandah

When the husband, after insertion and penetration, raises the legs of his wife, who still lies upon her back, and joins her thighs closely together.

Vinaka-tiryak-bandha

When the husband, placing himself alongside of his wife, raises one of his legs over her hip and leaves the other lying upon the bed or carpet.

Samputa-tiryak-bandha

When both man and woman lie straight upon their sides, without any movement or change in the position of their limbs.

Karkata-tiryak-bandha

When both being upon their sides, the husband lies between his wife's thighs, one under him, and the other being thrown over his flank, a little below the breast.

Padm-asana

The husband in this favorite position sits cross-legged upon the bed or carpet, and takes his wife upon his lap, placing his hands upon her shoulders.

Upapad-asana

Whilst both are sitting, the woman slightly raises one leg by placing her hand under it, and the husband enjoys her.

Vaidurit-asana

The husband embraces his wife's neck very closely, and she does the same to him.

Phanipash-asana

The husband holds his wife's feet, and the wife those of her husband.

Sanyaman-asana

The husband passes both the legs of his wife under his arms at the elbow, and holds her neck with his hands.

Yugmapad-asana

Is a name given by the poets to that position in which the husband sits with his legs wide apart, and, after insertion and penetration, presses the thighs of his wife together.

Vinarditasana

A form possible only to a very strong man with a very light woman; he raises her by passing both her legs over his arms at the elbow, and moves her about from left to right, but not backwards or forwards, till the supreme moment arrives.

Markatasana

Is the same position as Vinarditasana; in this, however the husband moves the wife in a straight line away from his face, that is, backwards and forwards, but not from side to side.

Knee and elbow standing-form

A posture which also requires great bodily strength in the man. Both stand opposite to each other, and the husband passes his two arms under his wife's knees, supporting her upon the inner elbows; he then raises her as high as his waist, and enjoys her, whilst she must clasp his neck with both her hands.

Hari-vikrama-utthita-bandha

The husband raises only one leg of his wife, who with the other stands upon the ground.

Kirti-utthita-bandha

This requires strength in the man. The wife, clasping her hands and placing her legs round her husband's waist, hangs, as it were, to him, whilst he supports her by placing his forearms under her hips.

The cow posture

The wife places herself upon all fours, supported on her hands and feet (not her knees), and the husband approaching from behind, falls upon her waist, and enjoys her as if he were a bull. There is much religious merit in this form.

Elephant posture

The wife lies down in such a position that her face, breast, stomach, and thighs all touch the bed or carpet. The husband, extending himself upon her, and bending himself like an elephant, with the small of the back much drawn in, works underneath her, and effects insertion.

Contrary position

The wife lies straight upon her outstretched husband with her breast being applied to his bosom; she presses his waist with her hands, and moving her hips sharply in various directions, enjoys him.

Like the large bee

The wife, having placed her husband at full length upon the bed or carpet, sits at squat upon his thighs, closes her legs firmly after she has effected insertion; and, moving her waist in circular form, churning, as it were, enjoys her husband, and thoroughly satisfies herself.

Utthita-uttana-bandha

The wife, whose passion has not been gratified by previous copulation, should make her husband lie upon his back, and sitting cross-legged upon his thighs, should seize his lingam [penis], effect insertion, and move her waist up and down, advancing and retiring; she will derive great comfort from this process.

F: Often I've fantasized about doing it while riding in the carriages around Central Park in New York.

F: I don't have a horse and buggy, but in a car you can do this one with the seat all the way back and your feet on the dashboard.

F: That horse looks a wee bit jealous. . . .

M: Is this the equivalent of a '57 Chevy?

F: Feeling your man inside but not really seeing him
does let your mind wander to all sorts of
interesting things—like fantasizing that
you are with Jean-Claude van Damme!

F: Like this one for a change. But I don't like to
turn my back completely on my lover.

F: This one's very sensuous.

F: Sitting on top of the world.

Selected Positions

from the

Ishimpo

by

Tamba Yasuyori

These descriptions are loose adaptations from the *Ishimpo* translation in *The Tao of Sex* by Howard S. Levy and Akira Ishihara.

The dragon turns over
With the female lying down on her back, the male lies on top of her with his thighs pressing on the mat, the female raises her vagina to receive the jade stalk, he moves about leisurely, eight shallow followed by two deep, and repeating.

The tiger's tread
The female faced downwards in a crawling position, her buttocks up and head down, the male kneels behind her and embraces her belly. Then he inserts his jade stalk and penetrates deeply.

The monkey springs
The male is kneeling, and the female lies on her back with her thighs on his shoulders. Her buttocks and lower back are raised.

Cicada affixed
With the female lying front downwards, the male kneels behind and inserts his jade stalk deeply into her vagina.

The tortoise mounts
The female lies on her back with her knees bent to her chest. While pushing her feet towards her breasts, the male inserts his jade stalk deeply and follows with both deep and shallow strokes.

The phoenix flutters
The female lies on her back with her knees bent and thighs pointing upward. The male crawls between her thighs and deeply inserts his jade stalk.

A rabbit sucking a hair
The male lies flat on his back, extending his legs. Facing his feet, the female straddles him, her knees to the outside.

Fish with scales joined
The male lies on his back, extending his legs. Facing his head, the female straddles him, her knees to the outside. The female moves so as to prolong her pleasure.

Cranes with necks intertwined
The male sits in a squatting position with the female facing him and straddling his thighs, she embraces his neck while he embraces her buttocks and assists her hip movements.

Silkworm reeling silk
The female is on her back and after the male inserts the jade stalk, she entwines both legs around his back and embraces the man's neck.

Shifting-turning dragon
The female lies on her back with both legs bent up, the male kneels at the female's thighs and with his left hand pushes both of her ankles upward and forward. He then inserts the jade stalk into the jade gate with his right hand.

Fish eye to eye
The male and the female lie down on their side face to face, and the female places one leg over the man. They suck each other's mouths and sip each other's tongues.

Sky-soaring butterfly
The man is on his back with both legs extended, and the female squats on top of him face to face. Then she advances with her hands his male tip into the jade gate.

The seagull soars
Standing beside the bed, the male lifts the female's legs onto his shoulders and inserts his jade stalk. Depending on the height of the bed the females upper back or neck and shoulders rest on the bed.

The horse's shaking hooves
The female is lying on her back, and the male lifts one of her legs onto his shoulder and inserts his jade stalk deeply.

Mountain goat facing a tree
The male sits with his legs extended, and the female straddles his thighs, facing his feet. The female then lowers her head and observes the insertion of the jade stalk while the male embraces her waist.

The donkey of early, mid, and late spring
Standing, the female bends forward, resting her hands on the bed or floor. The male stands behind, holding her waist with his hands, and inserts the jade stalk into the jade gate.

F: Deep penetration. Good.

F: Both partners can be quite active in this position, and it's delightful playing with up-and-down versus forward-and-backward motions . . . each giving their own juicy sensations.

F: This is our favorite position for tantric manifestation. My partner uses essential oils of rose and ylang ylang on my back. Then we build the energy for release while I open my being to be a channel for the energy of manifestation and send the energy out the top of my head to my intent.

M: Going to try that one too!

India Temple Walls

Today a sculpture of coital embrace at the entrance of a modern church, synagogue, or temple would be considered the worst heresy possible.

Yet in India between about the ninth and thirteenth centuries, temples appeared adorned with some of the finest erotic sculpture the world has known.

The illustration to the left depicts one of the remaining temple buildings at Konarak. From this aerial view, we see what appears to be a typical jungle temple withering from the storms of centuries. Nothing from this height suggests that as the worshiper approached and entered such religious structures, he or she saw life-size sculptures revealing a wide variety of sensual and sexual expressions, perhaps by deities, perhaps by humans, perhaps by beings from other realms. At the temples of Konarak, the eighty-five temples of Khajurajo, and elsewhere, hundreds of sculptures display our erotic nature with joy, tenderness, playfulness, and passion.

Ecstatic spirituality is very foreign to most of us. Sexuality on the sacred altar is incomprehensible for our mainstream Western religious thought. The following pages of images from the India temple walls suggest that at least some ancient lovers embraced the sacred and the sexual in a dance of ecstasy.

With such easy visual availability of such a variety of sexual positions for even the commonest of the populace, we might wonder if there were *any* sexual secrets for these ancient lovers.

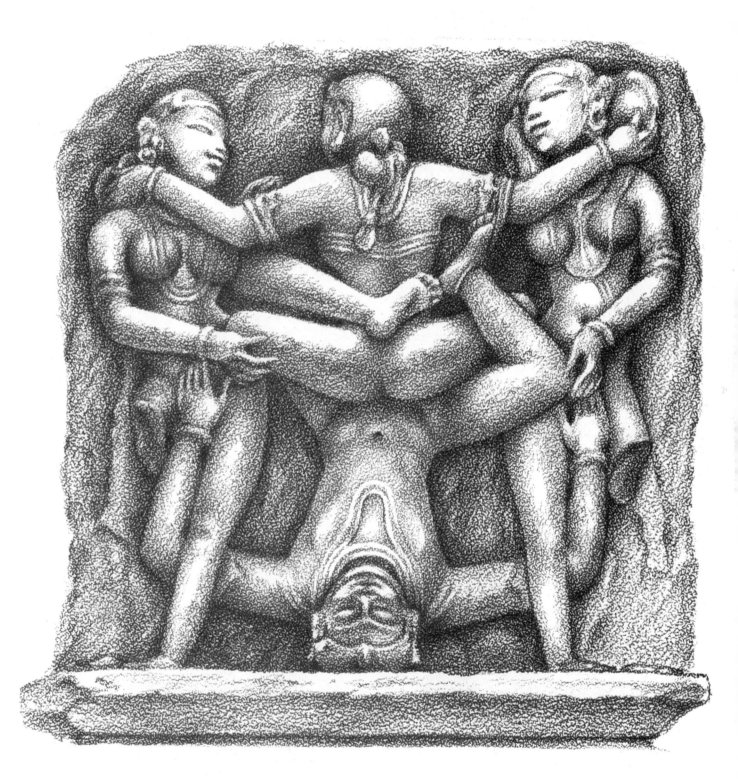

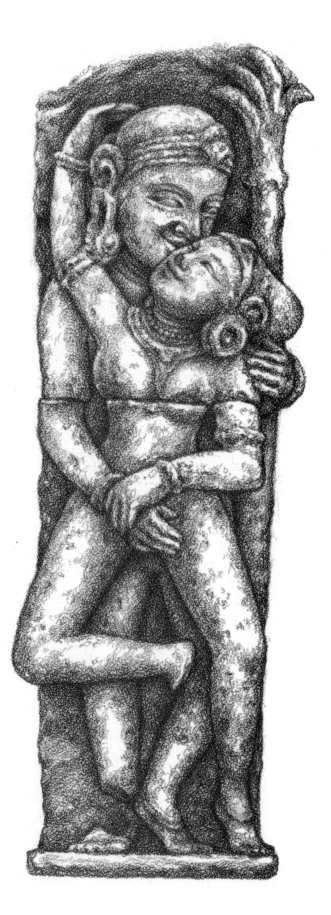

Japanese Shunga Art

Sex is natural and naturally enjoyable. This is the constant in most Japanese shunga art.

Translated literally, *shunga* means "spring drawings." In Japan between 1660 and 1860 in a flourishing artistic movement, accomplished artists created wood-block prints depicting uninhibited sex.

This was a culture where sex was not sin. While not portraying sex as mystical or spiritual as in the Tantric tradition in India and Tibet, much of the shunga art, however, presents sexual pleasure and sensual delight as inherent human nature. Because of the characteristic overly engorged penis in many prints, one might wonder though if the populace indeed worshiped a phallic god.

Revealing a variety of sexual positions, shunga art often emphasizes the experience of sensual and sexual pleasure in the moment. Lovers and groups of lovers express themselves, sometimes passionately, sometimes tenderly, but always without shame. The realm of the senses is to be appreciated—a theme in sharp contrast to the beliefs of the Puritans landing at Plymouth Rock shortly before the beginning of the art movement in Japan.

In the following illustrations, Kyle Spencer, the illustrator of this book, brings her experience as a modern artist to a contemporary adaptation of the sensual shunga style from a Shogun world.

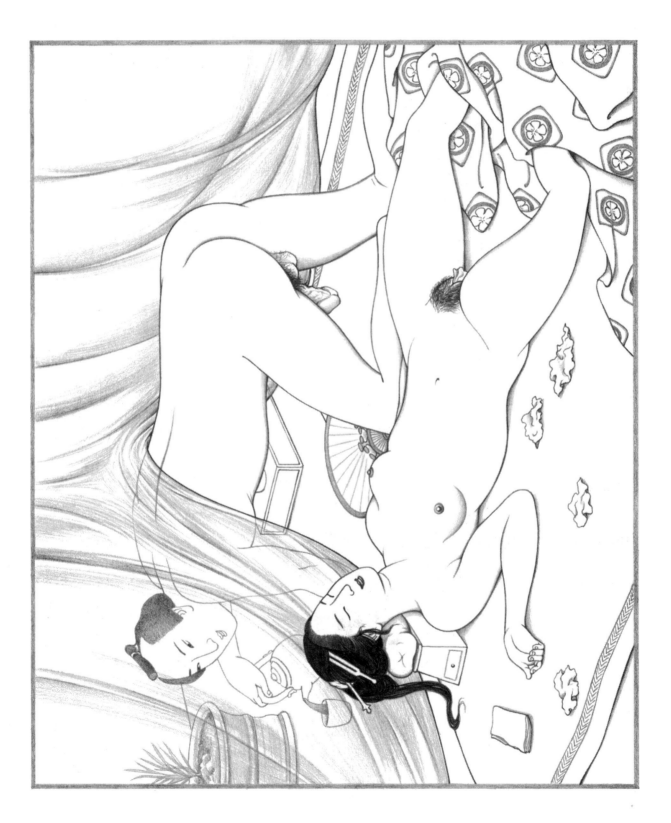

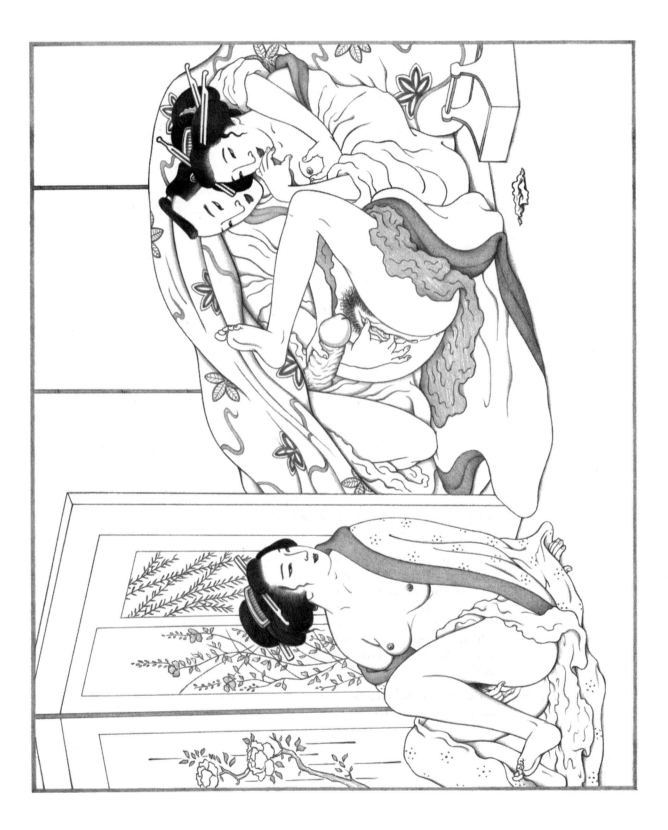

Appendix:
General Thoughts from Readers

In addition to writing about their experience of each position's illustration, several individuals and couples added their general feelings about viewing and trying out the various positions.

Most of the following quotes are from experienced meditators who embrace their sexuality fully. Their words are an indication of what we might learn from the ancient lovers.

Looking through, reading the text, and discussing (even laughing at) some of these positions in itself was a close, sensual experience, leading to touching and loving sexual encounters. Talking about the ideas led to opening up and expressing ideas of our own likes and dislikes—honest, sincere, and vulnerable.

I have to admit it's been fun jumping on my man in an unaccustomed way—taking him by surprise, so to speak.

We like to use our sexual release for manifestations. My partner at the moment of release receives a word or phrase. As I feel his energy enter me, I send the energy out the top of my head for the benefit of Self, our union, or the planet, depending on the message I receive in the moment.

Our sexuality is not only something that can be used for the enhancement of an intimate relationship, for physical pleasure, or for procreation; it can also be used for personal transformation, physical and emotional healing, self-realization, spiritual growth, and as a way to learn about all of life and death. An honest, focused, sexually knowledgeable and supportive person is a driving and extremely powerful force that can not only inspire his or her lover(s), but has the potential to contribute to the well-being of all life on earth.

My lover and I are not focused on positions but rather on energetics. We like to create energetic orbits around each other with energy descending the front chakras and ascending the back chakras, but always the orbit encompasses us both no matter the position.

About the Author and the Artist

The Author

Kenneth Ray Stubbs, Ph.D., is a certified sexologist and a certified masseur. Originally trained as a sociologist, he eventually studied and gave seminars and trainings in massage and sexuality both for the general public and sex therapists throughout North America and Europe. He has also taught as an adjunct faculty member at the Institute for the Advanced Study of Human Sexuality in San Francisco.

His interest in meditation led him to study with a variety of teachers from various traditions, most of which have a sex-positive approach or totally embrace sacred sexuality.

Secret Sexual Positions is the result of a personal blending of this study of Western social sciences and ancient meditation paths.

The Illustrator

Kyle Spencer is a freelance illustrator residing in Oakland, California. She has a bachelor's degree from the Academy of Art College in San Francisco. Her art also appears in *Erotic Massage*, *Tantric Massage*, and *The Clitoral Kiss*, as well as in *Tantra: The Magazine* and *Ecstasy Journal*.

Some Additional Reading

Texts by writers from the originating culture:

Bill Wahlberg, *Star Warrior: The Story of SwiftDeer*, Bear & Company. (See the appendix on Quodoushka.)

J. William Lloyd, *The Karezza Method, or Magnetation: The Art of Connubial Love*, Health Research.

Jolan Chang, *The Tao of Love and Sex: The Ancient Chinese Way to Love and Ecstasy*, E. P. Dutton.

Mantak Chia & Maneewan Chia, *Healing Love Through the Tao: Cultivating Female Sexual Energy*, Healing Tao Books.

Mantak Chia & Michael Winn, *Taoist Secrets of Love: Cultivating Male Sexual Energy*, Aurora Press.

Stephen T. Chang, *The Tao of Sexology: The Book of Infinite Wisdom*, Tao Publishing.

Translations of original texts:

Alain Danielou, *The Complete Kama Sutra: The First Unabridged Modern Translation of the Classic Indian Text*, Park Street Press.

Douglas Wile, *Art of the Bedchamber: The Chinese Sexual Yoga Classics Including Women's Solo Meditation Texts*, State University of New York Press.

Howard S. Levy and Akira Ishihara, trans., *The Tao of Sex: The Essence of Medical Prescriptions (Ishimpo)*, Integral Publishing.

Kalayana Malla, author, Richard F. Burton and F. F. Arbuthnot, trans., *Ananga Ranga, Stage of the Bodiless One: The Hindu Art of Love*, Medical Press of New York.

Sir Richard Burton and F. F. Arbuthnot, trans., Charles Fowkes, ed., *The Illustrated Kama Sutra, Ananga-Ranga, Perfumed Garden*, Park Street Press.

Sir Richard Burton, trans., Charles Fowkes, ed., *The Perfumed Garden*, Park Street Press.

Instructional books by modern Westerners:

David and Ellen Ramsdale, *Sexual Energy Ecstasy: A Practical Guide to Lovemaking Secrets of the East and West*, Bantam Books.

Jwala and Robb Smith, *Sacred Sex: Ecstatic Techniques for Empowering Relationships*, Mandala Books.

Kamala Devi, *The Eastern Way of Love: Tantric Sex and Erotic Mysticism*, Simon and Schuster.

Nik Douglas and Penny Slinger, *Sexual Secrets: The Alchemy of Ecstasy*, Destiny Books.

General references and readings:

Alan Watts, *Erotic Spirituality: The Vision of Konarak*, Collier Books.

Barbara G. Walker, *The Woman's Encyclopedia of Myths and Secrets*, HarperSan Francisco.

Georg Feuerstein, *Sacred Sexuality: Living the Vision of the Erotic Spirit*, Jeremy P. Tarcher.

Kenneth Ray Stubbs, ed., *Women of the Light: The New Sexual Healers*, Secret Garden. (Especially see chapters on the meditation teacher and the FireWoman.)

Kenneth Ray Stubbs, *Sacred Orgasms* of *The Tantric Massage Trilogy*, Secret Garden. (Compares Tantric, Taoist, and Quodoushka approaches.)

Ralph Metzner, *Maps of Consciousness*, Collier Books. (Excellent chapters on Tantra and Taoism.)

Rufus C. Camphausen, *The Encyclopedia of Erotic Wisdom: A Reference Guide to the Symbolism, Techniques, Rituals, Sacred Texts, Psychology, Anatomy, and History of Sexuality*, Inner Traditions International. (An excellent reference book.)

End Notes

1 Song of Songs 6:3.

2 Sir Richard Burton, trans., Charles Fowkes, ed., *The Perfumed Garden* (Rochester, VT: Park Street Press, 1992), p. 11.

3 Ibid., p. 10.

4 Modern-day translation of Song of Songs verse. Source unknown.

5 Diane Wolkstein and Samuel Noah Kramer, *Inanna: Queen of Heaven and Earth* (New York: Harper & Row, 1983), various selections.

6 See, for example, James George Frazer, *The Golden Bough*, Book I, Chapter 7, in various editions and abridgments. Also see Samuel Noah Kramer, *The Sacred Marriage Rite* (Bloomington: Indiana University Press, 1969).

7 "Ban on Nude Dancing Backed by High Court," *Los Angeles Times*, Home Ed., 22 June 1991, pt. A, p. A-1.

8 "So the LORD our God delivered into our hands Og also, the king of Bashan, and all his people . . . and we took all his cities at that time . . . threescore cities . . . utterly destroying the men, women, and children, of every city." [Deuteronomy 3:3–6]

9 "And the booty, being the rest of the prey which the men of war had caught, was six hundred thousand and seventy thousand and five thousand sheep, and threescore and twelve thousand beeves, and threescore and one thousand asses, and thirty and two thousand persons in all, of women that had not known man by lying with him." [Numbers 31:32–35]
   See *When God Was a Woman* by Merlin Stone (New York: Harvest/ Harcourt Brace Jovanovich, 1976) for an extensive discussion of the early Hebrews and the surrounding sex-positive cultures.

10 See Elinor W. Gadon, *The Once and Future Goddess* (New York: HarperCollins, 1989), p. 113, and Starhawk, *Dreaming the Dark*, new edition (Boston: Beacon Press, 1982, 1988), p. 187.

11 Sir Richard Burton and F. F. Arbuthnot, trans., Charles Fowkes, ed., *The Illustrated Kama Sutra, Ananga-Ranga, Perfumed Garden* (Rochester, VT: Park Street Press, 1991), p. 18.

12 Ibid., p. 68.

[13] Sir Richard Burton, trans., Charles Fowkes, ed., *The Perfumed Garden* (Rochester, VT: Park Street Press, 1992), p. 32.

[14] Howard S. Levy and Akira Ishihara, trans., *The Tao of Sex* (Lower Lake, CA: Integral Publishing, 1989), p. 17.

[15] J. William Lloyd, *The Karezza Method* (1931), from an underground reprinting sometime in the 1970s, p. 31.

[16] Dr. Stephen T. Chang, *The Tao of Sexology: The Book of Infinite Wisdom* (San Francisco: Tao Publishing, 1986), p. 27.

[17] There are only three other publicly published materials on Quodoushka, to my knowledge, available at this time. Appendix C in Bill Wahlberg's biography of Harley SwiftDeer Reagan, *Star Warrior: The Story of SwiftDeer*, is on Quodoushka (Santa Fe: Bear & Company, 1993). In *Women of the Light: The New Sexual Healers*, Stephanie Rainbow Lightening Elk describes her experiences as a Quodoushka practitioner (Larkspur, CA: Secret Garden, 1997, Kenneth Ray Stubbs, ed.). In my *Sacred Orgasms* of *The Tantric Massage Trilogy*, I share more of my Quodoushka experiences (Larkspur, CA : Secret Garden, 1998).

[18] Grandfather Tom Two Bears Wilson was president of the Navaho Native American Church until his death.

Acknowledgments

Secret Sexual Positions has been almost ten years in the making. When I first sat down to write this book, *Sacred Orgasms* (now a part of the *Tantric Massage Trilogy*) came out instead. Since then, many people have contributed to the new outcome.

Creating a feeling far from a porn-genre tone was crucial for my intent with *Secret Sexual Positions*. Kyle Spencer, the illustrator, indeed is able to show us the fun, the joy, and the intimacy sex can be. She brings such a soft sensuality to the images, adding a communication that beautifully conveys the underlying messages I attempt with the written word. I am deeply grateful for her abilities and support. The four different illustration styles used here span almost a decade of her artistic development.

Richard Stodart, another accomplished artist, has creatively developed this book's cover and contributed significantly to the layout design. I am honored by his friendship and artistic inspiration.

Several individuals were instrumental in advising which sexual positions to include. SwiftDeer, Jwala, and Louise-Andrée Saulnier played principal roles. Also, often I gave Kyle a free hand in selecting from the myriad of photographs and illustrations from many different sources. I told her, "Let's have fun with this book."

Originally for commentary on the positions, I sought "quotable quotes" from experienced sacred-sex meditators. After several friends and relatives said they too would like to comment on those "crazy fucking positions," I opened the gates. Among those who gave quotes are Cree Powell, Jonathan Hamilton, Porsche Lynn, Kathleen Kent, Tim and Linda Smith, Mary Sennawald, Chip Costello, Nancie Ennis, Storm Catcher, Annie Sprinkle, Michael Stein and friends, Lewis Irving and students, Richard Lockwood, Danielle and Cliff Berrien, Yvonne and Greg Carleton, Patricia Hursh, and Victor Shamas.

Inspiration and support to complete this book came from numerous friends and sources. Chyrelle Chasen and Sandy Trupp have been my cheerleaders. Rick van Genderen, another artist, was very supportive in the early days. Jessica Martinez and *Kama Sutra*, the movie, turned on the juices when my motivation was low. Jack Weatherford, author of *Indian Givers*, sent a valuable e-mail confirming Balboa's atrocities. Nancie Ennis, my secretary, has kept my office burdens low. Nancy Carleton, my copyeditor, is always so easy to work with, saving me many an embarrassment. And much thanks to Danielle Berrien for her nurturing support.

Also by Kenneth Ray Stubbs

Erotic Massage
The Touch of Love
ISBN 0-939263-02-5

"Superbly illustrated. . . . The techniques described are simple, easy to perform. . . . The book is clearly illustrated and proceeds in a formal fashion to give the lay-person a truly alive experience of massage therapy."
Massage Magazine

"The drawings are explicit yet artful; the text takes a tender, playful, yet respectful tone, and instructions are clear without sounding clinical."
Medical Self Care

Erotic Massage Video
Complete Edition
ISBN 0-939263-13-5

"Soft lighting and shadows, undulating music and curves of glistening flesh complete the ambiance. . . . Direct genital stimulation transforms the sensual experience from relaxation to higher levels of sexual arousal. Compared to the typically crude and unromantic antics of X-rated videos, this stands out as sensual/sexual artistry. A fitting portrayal of the beauty of massage."
Ecstasy Journal

"They play these bodies as a concert pianist caresses his grand piano."
Libido

Romantic Interludes
A Sensuous Lovers Guide
ISBN 0-939263-14-9

"Here is a book that is a pleasure to read and to recommend. It is a book for all adults who want a guide that will help them develop the art of loving touch and a sensitive and intimate way of relating to that significant person in their life. Human beings are born sexual, but we are not born lovers. . . . Know of no other book available that is as clear and well-written."
SIECUS Report

The Clitoral Kiss
A Fun Guide to Oral Sex for Men and Women
ISBN 0-939263-08-4

"Here's a book that's so much fun you'll quickly get over any inhibitions you may have felt. . . . Whether the subject is oral aerobics, or any one of more than two dozen kissing, sucking, and licking games. Stubbs and Chasen never forget that sex is play, not geometry. Hey, who ever said that you have to be serious all the time?"
The Millennium Whole Earth Catalog

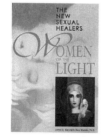

Women of the Light
The New Sexual Healers
ISBN 0-939263-12-2

"A truly radical book, one that documents living women . . . in surprising and moving ways."
American Library Association's
Booklist

"Fascinating and highly readable book makes the convincing case that sexwork . . . can be a source of sexual healing, psychological growth, and spiritual awareness."
Whole Earth Review

Erotic Massage

TWO VOLUMES
Now Available In
ONE
VIDEO!

Designed to complement the step-by-step instruction in the *Erotic Massage* book, this educational video demonstrates the gentleness, the respect, the grace of the strokes integrated into a total experience. In easy-to-learn strokes, you and your partner can bring together the sensual, the erotic, and the intimate.

NOTICE: This is an explicit, two-volume video. Nudity and genital massage are shown. What you will see is sensitive, caring massage for the whole body in the privacy of your home.

VOLUME ONE: the back, the feet, the neck, the face, and more—all the strokes in the book except the genital massage, in the same order as in the book.

VOLUME TWO: the female and male genital massage as in the book, plus new, unwritten strokes.

For Private Home Use Only.
VHS / Hi-Fi Stereo / Color / 60 Minutes